the bible

the bible

an anthology of personal essays and narratives about bisexuality

Edited by
Lauren Nickodemus & Ellen Desmond
With a foreword by Lauren James

Published in the UK in 2017 by
Monstrous Regiment Publishing
Edinburgh, Scotland
editor@monstrous-regiment.com
www.monstrous-regiment.com

Distributed in the UK by
Monstrous Regiment Publishing

Cover design by ELEMdesign

ISBN: 978-1-5272-1192-6

Printed and bound in Great Britain by Clays Ltd, Elcograf S.p.A.

THE BIBLE: *An Anthology of Personal Narratives and Essays about Bisexuality* was crowdfunded on Kickstarter by 200 people who believe in the importance of this work and its contribution to wider social conversation. It consists of essays, carefully selected from a pool of submissions, by authors who pitched topics they feel are relevant to a discussion on bisexuality. While compiling the anthology, we made best efforts to provide an intersectional, original and varied spread of narratives and experiences from people based in transatlantic locations. However, there are limitations to any work of this size, and reach always needs to be expanded upon.

While self-identifying bisexuals are the focus of this anthology, it also includes some experiences from people of other identifications. For example, it includes outlooks from pansexuals, homosexual panromantics, people who once identified as bisexual but no longer do, and many who identify simply as queer. As editors, we believe it is important not to exclude the voice of anyone who feels they relate to the marginalisation of bisexuality within the LGBTQ+ community.

For consistency, throughout the book we use the term LGBTQ+ when referring to the vibrant queer community. We know this isn't the only label that fits, and it might not be your label, but we have used it following many conversations with LGBTQ+ people in the hope of maximum inclusion, and minimum exclusion.

We would like to alert readers that some essays contain potentially triggering content, particularly in the areas of sexual assault and rape (*Sexual Assault and Gender*, page 15), and self-harm and suicide (*Photographs*, page 23, and *FML: Fix My Life*, page 141).

This anthology is simply a selection of 20 voices – a mere line in a story that is nowhere near completely documented yet. But we hope it will, at the very least, inspire more people to speak, and even more people to listen.

Ellen Desmond
Lauren Nickodemus
November 2017

contents

contents

foreword

by Lauren James

When I was asked to write a foreword for this anthology, I was unsure at first. What did I have to say about bisexuality? I've not studied gender and sexuality, nor read many books on the subject. I didn't feel like I had the experience necessary to contribute, beyond being bisexual myself. I felt like I needed some way to justify my decision to stand up and represent an identity. And on reading the essays in this collection, I think that's something that a lot of bisexual people face: the feeling that you're not quite allowed this. That you have to be willing to fight for your place in the LGBTQ+ community.

Bisexual people don't live passively: they work to be seen, heard and noticed every day. It takes confidence, determination, bravery and belief to be able to out yourself not only to straight people but also to other LGBTQ+ people. To provide proof that you are both: not just one or the other, straight or gay.

This community is one of strength, and that strength is visible on every page of this collection. LBGTQ+ people are often denied a history of happy endings, of people like us living full and rich lives. Role models are vital in showing children and adults alike the path forward. As Chitra Ramaswamy says in her essay, 'sometimes, because there are so few role models, so little understanding and so much bafflement, you don't really know who you love'. Autobiographical accounts like the ones in this book help to fill the dearth of heroes available to LGBTQ+ people. By providing examples of real people, it reassures readers that your experiences are valid and you are not alone. You matter. You can stand proud amongst a whole community of people just like you.

The range and breadth of experiences in this book prove that there's no 'right' way to be bisexual – that you don't need to have a list of past and present relationships ready to offer as evidence of your identity. This book doesn't represent every bisexual experience, because, of course, that would be impossible. But it does highlight significant moments in the journeys of real bisexual people in ways that apply to the few as well as the many. Whether you see yourself reflected in these pages, or only catch a glimpse of your own experiences in the stories told, I hope that you find something reassuring in hearing the outspoken voices of a people who so often live silently.

Bisexuality is a diverse identity that can so often stay invisible, or pass as straight in the real world. But as this book shows, bisexual people are here. We aren't going anywhere. And we've got quite a lot to say. Authors, write us into your stories. Queer communities, represent us with more than just the 'B' in LGBTQ+. Schools, teach us in your classes. Employers, make safe spaces for your workers.

We need it: bisexual people have the highest levels of depression, anxiety, self-harm and suicide of any LGBTQ+ identity, are the least likely to come out at work, and experience more identity confusion as teenagers than gay and lesbian peers.[1] These essays go a long way toward explaining why that might be the case – as well as showing the joys and positive side of being bisexual in the twenty-first century.

As a writer, I try to make sure that all of my books accurately represent the rich diversity of the real world I live in, because those are the books I am most interested in reading. I write for a teenage audience, and I'm always aware that my books might be the first time a reader has seen a character of a certain identity in fiction, or that they might have only read examples of stereotypical, thinly drawn characters before. As Sarah Barnard says in her essay, 'I had to "decide" that characters from my favourite works of fiction were bi, because otherwise, my sexuality wouldn't be represented at all'. Non-fiction books like this essay collection, which show the varied and intersectional lives of real LGBTQ+ people, can only help fiction to become more diverse – and give those characters fulfilling lives and stories beyond a tragic coming out narrative.

You'll find a huge variety of experiences in these pages, whether that's related to fiction (*Sarah Barnard, page 87, Mel Reeve, page 131, and Lauren Vevers, page 43*), activism (*Laura Clay, page 99, and Viola Orson, page 105*), health (*Eleanor Reid, page 23, and Alice T, page 59*), religion (*Dany Carter, page 151*) or intersectionality (*Naomi Carroll, page 85, Joseph Guthrie, page 141, and Jayna Tavarez, page 117*). Whether you're a long-time student of gender and sexuality, or an amateur, like me, I guarantee you'll learn something from the experiences discussed within this book.

If you are just entering the often confusing world of LGBTQ+ identities, I encourage you to visit the websites, articles and books cited in these essays, to continue your journey by exploring all of the varied and wonderful areas of this community. I promise you will find the place you belong, even if right now it feels like you never will.

Lauren James
October 2017

going either way

by Chitra Ramaswamy

YOU ARE 25 years old. Slap bang in the middle of your twenties, in the whirling middle of life it seems, though really adulthood is still only just beginning. You live alone in Glasgow, renting a flat from a friend of a friend in Woodlands; an area of faded grandeur like so many in that great and deprived city. Mostly occupied by students and Scottish-Pakistani families (you are neither but could be mistaken for both), it's a place where abandoned and soon sodden sofas line the streets and the sandstone tenements are bedeviled with cracks. Living alone is both a thrill and a fright. You revel in being the only person with a set of keys and worry about how you will remove spiders all by yourself. (You won't: on one shameful occasion you will see one in the bathroom, hurl your old *Norton Anthology of Literature* from your Glasgow University days at it, miss, and end up washing at the kitchen sink for three days.)

It is the first time you have lived alone and though you do not know it, you have not lived alone again since. And so this period has taken on the shimmering and slightly warped patina that comes with being a one-off in life so far. To you, more than a decade later, it seems like a charmed life, a hallowed moment in which all the things that have not yet happened are waiting, quietly, to materialise. Whenever you picture this little flat with its pocked and poorly painted white floors and the radiators that get too hot, too quick, you are reminded of that time. Of late night takeaways eaten alone in bed while watching back to back episodes of *Sex and the City*. Of the neighbour, whom you never met, practising his saxophone on weekend mornings. Of the reassuring yet melancholy feeling, familiar to those who live alone, of arriving home and finding everything precisely as you left it. And of the unexpected metamorphosis that takes place within you while you live there: from loving a man to loving a woman. From being a straight woman to a bisexual woman, though really in hindsight you were always the latter. From inhabiting two minority statuses – Indian in Britain, English in Scotland – to three. A change that, like so many of the most profound transformations in life, was there all along. Not really a change at all, then, it's just that it went unnamed before.

For now, you are in a long distance relationship with a man. You met during university, fell madly in love, and were inseparable for five years. He has moved to London and soon he will move further still, to China. Already you both sense the relationship is in its last throes, though you do not speak of it. Instead you spend heady, slightly edgy weekends together in the city where you met, then see him off on the train to London, where you (not he) are from, and weep alone on the platform under the glorious glass roof of Central Station. This life suits you. Even the pining has its pleasures.

Then there is your boss at work, with whom you go drinking on Tuesday nights after putting to bed the weekly magazine you edit together. You talk for hours while drinking Peroni straight from the bottle in a Glasgow bar with scuffed black and white chequered floors and tarnished mirrors on the walls. Your boss, a lesbian, is in a long-term relationship with another woman. You privately think how nice it must be to not have to always put the toilet seat down, a minor battle constantly and wordlessly fought in so many hetero homes. You have never been with a woman before. You imagine it to be soft, sympathetic, fun.

And so it happens. You begin to realise on weekends that you can't wait for Monday to come around again and that this is curious, unexpected, the wrong way round. Tuesday nights become the highlight of your week: talking to this small bright woman so different from you, witnessing your beliefs, interests, senses of humour, and lives become entwined. You are dreamy, distracted. You feel constantly furtive and amused as though you are harbouring a secret from yourself. Indeed, you are, for you are falling in love. You would recognise the signs immediately if the object of your desire were a man.

You are 30 years old and have moved fifty miles east to Edinburgh with your partner of five years. The same woman, the only one you have loved. You share a mortgage, a dying profession (journalism), and a passion for Pedro Almodovar films and the ancient widescreen landscapes of northwest Scotland. Your lives are thickly interwoven now; your CD doubles (The Gotan Project, Ella Fitzgerald) tucked next to each other in the sideboard you spotted together in a secondhand shop. Your parents, friends, and colleagues all know and love your partner. You have come out and, like all LGBTQ+ people, will do so continuously, haphazardly, proudly, and painfully for the rest of your life. You are bisexual, but everyone who knows you assumes you are a lesbian and those who don't assume you are straight. One gay male friend confesses that he came out as bi to cushion the blow for his family 'because that's what we do, isn't it?' and you say nothing about his assumption that you must be the same. Another friend, telling you about a mutual acquaintance who has begun a romance with another woman after a long-term relationship with a man, describes her as a lesbian. 'Maybe she's bisexual,' you suggest, in hope, because it would be nice on occasion to find someone, somewhere who identifies as you do. 'Does it really matter?' the friend replies. Yes, it does, to you. When you do take the trouble to point out that you are, in fact, bisexual – that no matter whether you are with a man or a woman you will always have the potential to go either way – people look at you with scepticism, confusion, disbelief, or perhaps even envy. Their faces say this: you're lying to yourself, it's just a phase, you don't know what you want, you're letting the side down, you're greedy, you don't exist. But you do exist. Here you are.

You start to understand that this is what bi-erasure, an ironically conspicuous term in every article and discussion you come across about bisexuality, means. This is what it feels like to be invisible: the B lurking in the shadows between the G and the T, the one sexuality in whom few seem to believe but which, surely, is the one silently, even unknowingly, inhabited by the most. You voice this sense of fitting in nowhere, of being a kind of sexual nomad, to no one. You barely even notice it yourself, because this, too, is the consequence of inhabiting an identity deemed untrustworthy, unsafe. The kind that results in long pieces in *The New York Times Magazine* entitled 'The Scientific Quest to Prove Bisexuality Exists'. The kind that leads to an episode of *Girls* in which it's remarked that bisexuals are one of two groups that 'you can still make fun of' (the other being Germans). Or, back to *Sex and the City* again – that equally adored and derided cornerstone of Noughties female sexuality – in which bisexuality is described (by Carrie) as a 'layover on the way to Gaytown' or (by Miranda) as nothing more than 'greedy double-dipping'. Even Samantha, that blonde bastion of sexual liberation, writes bisexuality off as mere youthful sexual experimentation.

For you, though, it is not experimentation. It is a choice, a capacity, a state of ever-present potentiality: to love people for themselves. It is not a 50/50 split but a constantly moving, evasive target. Bisexuality, for you, is not about loving men and women the same, but about loving difference: because men and women are different just as each man or woman is different from the next man or woman. But sometimes, because there are so few role models, so little understanding and so much bafflement, you don't really know who you love. You find yourself thinking you ought to choose: society wants you to pick a side. But you can't. You don't want to. Why should anyone have to choose?

You are 38. You have two children and a dog with your partner of 13 years. The same woman, the only one you have ever loved. Your mortgage is ever so slightly smaller now. You have whittled down your CDs and acquired, as parents are wont to do, an offensive collection of battery operated plastic toys. You have replaced travel with family visits to London and culture with box-sets. Your partner has seen you give birth and you have seen her grieve the death of her father. You have had a civil partnership in the same draughty old building in Leith where your children's births have been registered. Equal marriage has come in but you have chosen not to 'upgrade'.

You are still and will always be bisexual, but like all long-worn and slightly frayed identities, you say it out loud less now. And bisexuality, too, has changed: the moving target shifted again. There are other identities, which were always there but had not been named, jostling for space and recognition. In an era of sexual fluidity, bisexuality seems anachronistic: defined by dualism in a world where there are now multiplicities. Its very existence is still debated nonetheless. And you are still perceived as a lesbian, as though your past has been written off, as though loving men was the exception, as though the present is all that ever counts.

Over the years, as you have grown into yourself, the beauty of bisexuality has dawned on you. Your sexuality, slowly, marvellously, has begun to suit you. Bisexuality, you now realise, is a permanent state of flux, a liminal space where you can be either/or, but you can also be neither/nor. It is not about sexual curiosity or whose genitals you prefer: rather it is a commitment to open-mindedness. You now feel there is an intoxicating liberty and privilege in ricocheting between the sexes, particularly now that parenting has anchored you more to your partner, your children, your home, dog, a certain way of life that you're not sure you entirely chose, and this small piece of land that is constantly debating its independence. You have discovered that the middle is a surprisingly edgy place to be. Living here requires bravery, which is why research shows that 80% of bisexuals end up in straight relationships. Sometimes the desire to conform can outstrip all others.

You are struck by the comparison with the unsettled way you have always inhabited your race: that same sense of being simultaneously too brown and not brown enough. In India too British, in Britain too Indian. Perhaps this is why you, a Londoner born of first-generation Indian immigrants, have ended up in Scotland. You seem to thrive in places where you are even more of an outsider. The truth is, you have never really fitted in anywhere, neither in gay bars nor Hindu temples, and this is both as it is and, increasingly with age, as you like it. So this is what it means for you, at 38, to be bisexual. You have chosen (or, if you prefer, been chosen by) an unfixed, untitled, and shape-shifting identity. One that by definition resists categorisation. Instead it commands flexibility, restlessness, the endless possibility of change. It is about who you are – racially, politically, socially, and person-ally – as much as who you love. Bisexuality may be the most invisible of the sexual identities, and invisibility is toxic in almost every way, but it has a single advantage. It means you can forge your own path, be whatever you want, love whoever you choose, exist in the shadows. For you, right now, bisexu-ality means freedom.

decline to answer:
why i'm making my 'invisible' bisexuality your business

by Lisa-Marie Ferla

IT IS JUNE 2011. I've been in my new job for three months – a return, after two and a half years, to the profession I was made redundant from when the crash came in 2008. There's a company-wide email: an annual diversity monitoring survey, done in conjunction with a trade publication. The usual stuff. Age bracket. Marital status. Gender identity. Disability. Educational background. Sexual orientation.

25-34

Married

Female

Not that you'd notice

State school

Decline to answer

I have, at this point, been married to my husband for almost a year. I tell myself that nobody wants to hear it.

I met my best friend in our first week of university. We bonded over having left school a year earlier than anybody else, and over our hatred of Catholic education. She had sung Madonna's 'Like A Virgin' until she got thrown out of Religious Education class, and had had an abortion. I would never have been so bold.

'I have something to tell you,' I called through a graffiti-covered bathroom stall door. We had been day-drinking again, because nobody ever checked your ID in the student union. 'I think I like girls, maybe.' It was the first time I had ever said it out loud.

My best friend dropped out of university; moved to London with a woman she had met on the internet. When I went to visit, my mum made me take my own towels.

I think she spent most of my time between boyfriends waiting for me to come out when I was a teenager. 'Is there anything you want to tell me?' she would say. I would look at her blankly, confused by the tremble in her voice. Then I would find a new boyfriend, and the tension – or that particular tension, at least; Catholic, remember? – would pass, and it was back to calling me downstairs whenever my 'pin-up' Courtney Love was on the telly.

My first TV crush... actually, no. My first TV crush was the appropriately-named Wesley Crusher, Will Wheaton's character in *Star Trek: The Next Generation*. He had floppy hair and cherry-coloured lips. Pre-pubescent cheekbones. He looked a little bit like me.

Eliza Dushku, Faith to Buffy's Vampire Slayer, was my second TV crush. She was also my boyfriend's. I'd go over to his house after work and we'd look at pictures of her online, me sitting squirming on his lap while we perched on his computer chair. We'd take late-afternoon naps, and I'd pretend to have sex dreams and let him touch me.

When I dumped him for my Friend Who Was a Boy, he made me take the vibrators and thong underwear he had bought me and that I had always refused to take home. 'I thought we'd get married,' he said. I threw the toys in the wheelie bin behind my mum's house on my way back in.

Months later, after I had twisted my Friend Who Was a Boy's arm long and hard enough to let me call him 'boyfriend', I asked him if he would see it as cheating if I kissed a woman.

'Of course,' he said. 'It *is* cheating.'

His answer genuinely surprised me.

There was never a defining moment of my bisexuality: no quiet realisation over the few fictional portrayals of LGBTQ+ characters around in the 1990s, no drunken kisses during which something fell into place. In retrospect, when you were raised to believe that 'sex is for a loving relationship in marriage', it didn't matter what gender you were fantasising about. It was still wrong.

There was at least one bumbling conversation in which I tried to explain to my mother that I wasn't bothered about whether I ended up with a man or a woman. 'Have you ever kissed a woman?' she gasped, terrified. 'Well, no,' I replied, as was the truth then. 'Then you're not gay,' she replied. I never tried again.

I never tried with anybody, honestly. I've never denied my sexuality, but I've never particularly performed it either. At its worst, it was the MySpace profile I set up shortly after my Friend Who Was a Boy broke up with me. I ticked 'divorced lesbian', because 'broken-hearted bisexual' felt too much like giving myself away and you didn't just...

not tick the boxes, not in those days. (Curiously enough, that MySpace profile was where I struck up a correspondence with the man who would become my husband.) More often, it was those diversity monitoring forms. 'None of your business,' I thought, furiously, as I filled in the 'decline to answer' box.

Why the reluctance? Because I have friends who have fought to have their relationships recognised by the law, by the state and by its institutions. The job centre and the NHS have looked through my friends' wives and partners. Nobody has ever attempted to undermine my marriage. Nobody has ever made me feel unsafe holding my husband's hand in the street, or resting my head on his shoulder on the night bus home.

Nobody needs to hear me boosting my social justice credentials while I don't have to live it.

There were a couple of reasons why that changed. The first came in June 2016, when the Iranian-American comedian Zahra Noorbakhsh came out on the first episode of her podcast, #GoodMuslimBadMuslim, that followed the murder of 49 people at the Pulse nightclub in Orlando by the terrorist Omar Mateen. For Noorbakhsh, coming out felt vital against a backdrop of right-wing American media eulogising one of its traditional bogeymen, LGBTQ+ people, as an opportunity to score points against radical Islam. And while my heart broke for one of my favourite comedians, I realised that for the first time I was listening to a woman of a similar age and whose relationship status was similar to my own stand up and say that she was part of a community in mourning.

Pulse was not my tragedy. I missed the 'nightclub' stage of young adulthood, so I never had that moment of clarity rubbing up against strangers in a dark, sweaty room where for the first time I felt that I was truly myself. At just-turned 34, I had never been able to be truly myself.

The second was a turning of the tide in bisexual visibility, specifically on social media. Critiques that the hashtag campaigns around Pride and National Coming Out Day allow allies to feel good about themselves while avoiding the physical and emotional labour of activism are often valid. But they've also provided me with the proof it turned out I needed that I'm not the only person wrestling with the conflict between her outwardly heteronormative life and her bisexual identity. Marrying my husband might appear, to those who seek to minimise bisexuality, as the ultimate in 'picking a side' – but I didn't pick a side. I picked a person.

Among the tired critiques of bisexual and pansexual-identifying people – that we're greedy, that we're hypersexualised, that we're feckless, that we're letting down one side or the other, that we're usurping queer identities in order to appear more interesting – the one that's always stung the most is this idea that we're not allowed to settle down. That my sexual attraction towards women in the abstract means that I will never feel completely fulfilled. It ignores the fact that people in heterosexual and homosexual couplings of all shapes and alignments experience sexual desire towards others all the time – that's just human nature. It doesn't mean you're going to jump on that other person on the bus or in the stationery cupboard, and it doesn't mean you love your partner any less.

It is June 2017, and I have just ticked the 'bisexual' orientation box on the annual diversity monitoring survey for the second year in a row.

Last year, when I self-identified as bisexual for the first time, I was a little nervous. But here are some things that didn't happen:

– the sky did not fall in;

– nobody from my work's HR turned up at my elbow for a quiet word;

– my computer cursor did not turn into a rainbow and start dancing around on the screen;

– the LGBTQ+ Police did not show up at my front door to arrest me for not being 'queer enough'.

Of course, ticking a box on an anonymous form is not the same as coming out, but those opportunities are tougher to find. I came out to my hairdresser as the Pride parade passed us last year. I humorously, but firmly, corrected a friend when the punchline of a joke he made turned on my attraction to men. My tribe is of the sympathetic sort for whom queerness is not a competition, and my sex life has never been the topic of family Christmas dinner chat.

I wrote this essay because my sexual orientation is as much a part of me as my gender identity, my blue eyes, my love of cats and my generalised anxiety disorder, and it's never been worth my while to hide any of those things either.

sexual assault and gender:
reflections on a double standard

by Codi Coday

USUALLY WHEN WE discuss sexual assault, the conversation begins and ends with examples of men assaulting women. However, sexual assault often happens in other gender combinations, and leaving these out of the central discussion is detrimental – especially to bisexual people.

Bisexuals are at the highest risk of sexual assault of any sexual orientation. In fact, one study in the US found that 61% of bisexual women and 47% of bisexual men have experienced some sort of intimate partner violence.[1] Unfortunately, bisexual people are in the unique position of being both more likely to experience sexual assault overall and more likely to experience 'unconventional' sexual assault* due to the fact that they often date more than one gender. I am one of the

---

* Unconventional sexual assault is any sexual assault that is not done by a man to a woman or that does not involve penile penetration into a vagina.

unlucky bisexual women who has experienced sexual assault by both a man and a woman on separate occasions. The actual moments of sexual assault were not all that different, but the aftermath of each deviated greatly. Sexual assault is dealt with completely differently when perpetrated by different genders: misogyny, biphobia, and the traditional ways in which sexual assault is discussed all play their part in this double standard.

At 18, I had been dating my college boyfriend for 9 months. He was the first person I really fell for, and we were infatuated with each other. Around this time I had developed a blood clot in my lung and my legs; I had an extremely close near death experience, and even on the brink of dying, all I could think about was seeing him again. So when a week later I was released from the hospital, I was ecstatic to hear that he was coming to visit me.

I left the hospital with a whopping dose of pain medication and stayed with my family to recover. At first, my boyfriend was wonderful and the fear I felt about my medical situation dissipated. But after my family went to bed that night, his behaviour shifted. He began to insist that now was the moment for us to have sex for the first time. It didn't matter that I said I didn't want to, that I was in too much pain, or that my parents were upstairs. He decided it was time, and what I wanted didn't matter.

It took a few months for it to click that I had been raped by someone I loved so dearly, and the timing could not have been worse. Dealing with nearly dying, severe medical issues, horrific pain, and now rape was too much to bear. The confusion didn't help either: how could I be raped by someone I sometimes wanted to have sex with, who I loved, who I thought loved me? To me, rape had always been something big scary men did to women who walked alone in dark alleys in the middle of the night. Naively, I had no clue it was something that could happen in a seemingly loving relationship.

Confused and heartbroken, I sought support from our friends. When I finally gained the courage to speak out, my friends did believe it had happened, but they determined it was somehow my fault. Even though I had been massively medicated to the point where I couldn't consent, and had clearly said no to boot, I 'must have sent the wrong signals'. They assumed I 'led him on', or equivocated, 'Well, you did say you wanted to have sex with him earlier in your relationship'. I ended up losing the majority of my friends; they all sided with him. He just seemed too nice to do something like that. I, in turn, was too dramatic because I refused to go to the same social gatherings as him, because I called it rape, because I insisted I had a right to be upset. I didn't bother reporting him. If I couldn't get my closest friends in the world to believe me and take me seriously, there was no way I could convince the police. I couldn't handle more people insisting it was my fault. I eventually had to transfer schools; my campus was notorious for siding with rapists and expecting victims to attend classes with them.

In the case of a man sexually assaulting a woman, our misogynistic society tends to believe that the assault occurred (as opposed to assaults between other genders, whose sexual activity is perceived as less legitimate) but often insists that it must have been the woman's fault. Victim blaming – that is, the view that assault is warranted or even deserved by the actions of the victim – is pervasive in today's culture. When we hear about cases of rape, the focus is put on the victim's appearance and behaviour, juxtaposed with concern over how a rape allegation could ruin the rapist's future. For example, take Brock Turner, a swimmer from Stanford who raped an unconscious woman.[2] The general public's reaction – as well as that of the designated judge – was to worry about his swimming career and future rather than condemn him for raping someone. The victim of his rape was criticised for what she was wearing, for drinking beforehand, and for not being more careful on a night out. Turner was released after only 3 months in jail, while the victim will deal with a lifetime of trauma. To see how common victim blaming is, all someone has to do is look at the comment section on any online article about sexual assault. In fact, in the comment section of news articles about sexual assault, 1 in 4 comments contain victim blaming.[3] It is also easy to find examples of this attitude in cases of sexual assault with high public visibility such as the Harvey Weinstein,[4] Bill Cosby,[5] or Donald Trump allegations.[6]

Three years after my first experience of assault, I came out as bisexual to my best friend of the time. When I did, she began to realise that she was bisexual as well, and that she was in love with me. I didn't share her feelings, but she claimed that we would still be able to remain close friends. Our friendship had some awkward road bumps, but mostly proceeded as normal. About a month later, we went to a party together, but left early because I was exhausted from cramming for midterms the week before. I fell asleep quickly in her spare bed when we got back to her place. Soon afterward, I was jolted awake. This time, it clicked automatically: I was being sexually assaulted by my cis female best friend. I shouted for her to stop, tried to get her off of me without getting violent; she was much smaller than I was, and even while she was hurting me I was still acutely aware that I didn't want to hurt *her*.

Her roommate was awake in the room adjacent. I screamed, over and over, but the roommate ignored me. She had hated me ever since I came out, and thought I was a bad influence on my best friend and had somehow turned her bisexual. She could have walked in and stopped the assault, but chose not to. Biphobia beat out human decency.

Again, after this, my ideas about sexual assault were deeply shaken. I understood that sexual assault could happen between people who were in a relationship, but I still never expected it to come from my best friend. I was even more shocked by the fact that I was raped by a woman. I never considered that women could rape people, or that being raped by a woman was a possible danger to consider.

Since this wasn't my first sexual assault, I knew how important it was to reach out for support. However, my biggest fear proved true: there was little support to be found. Overwhelmingly, when I told people I was raped by a woman, they insisted that it wasn't possible. Even my therapist wasn't helpful, as she had been when I was sexually assaulted by a man. In that instance, my therapist had acknowledged it wasn't my fault and worked with me on recovering from the trauma, never blaming me for what happened. This time, she chose to focus on the 'sexual dysfunction' of being bisexual rather than helping me recover from a similar trauma. I continued to try to find people to talk to among my friend group. Some refused to listen to me when I opened up because they 'didn't want to hear about my sex life with women'. Others I told claimed that if I had really been raped, I would have fought her enough to hurt her. Desperate, I turned to an online rape victims' support group. There, I had other sexual assault victims laugh at me or claim that my sexual assault was 'hot' – just because the gender of my rapist was different from that of theirs.

Sex between women is seen as less legitimate than sex that involves a penis and a vagina, while it is simultaneously hypersexualised and fetishised. Additionally, a disturbing number of people don't understand how sex between two cis women could work, which in turn leads to dangerous misconceptions about how sexual assault would work. Some people, like my best friend's roommate, don't fetishise sex between women, but see women who have sex with other women as either unable to be raped or deserving of rape.

These attitudes lead laypeople, police, and even therapists to refuse to acknowledge and recognise rape unless it includes a penis and penetration – which is a big problem for bisexuals. For me, these misconceptions certainly made it extremely difficult to get any support, even though the trauma endured was nearly the same when being raped by a woman as it was by a man. In both situations, I felt betrayed, violated, and guilty. I needed the same support, reassurance, and validation after both sexual assaults. However, support fell short in both situations – just for different reasons.

This problem doesn't just apply to my situation. A lot of people don't think it is possible for a woman to rape anyone or for a man to be raped. Non-binary and trans people are often left out of the conversation altogether. But the thing is, any gender can be sexually assaulted, and any gender can commit sexual assault. What people fail to comprehend is that *rape is about power, not sex*, and the power struggle is not dependant on what genders the sexual assault occurs between.

Being left out of the discussion about sexual assault has real repercussions for victims. 'Unconventional' sexual assault victims have trouble getting support from medical professionals, loved ones, lawyers, and therapists. That support is sometimes the only thing that gets victims through each day. Without adequate support, there is a real danger of PTSD, medical problems due to untreated injuries, depression, anxiety, and suicide. I suspect it is no coincidence that bisexuals have higher rates of all of the above considering how likely it is for them to experience sexual assault.

I didn't understand that rape could come from any gender, and from any type of relationship, until these two experiences happened to me – as they do to so many other bisexuals. But people shouldn't have to go through a sexual assault to understand that the victims of it, raped by any gender, all need to be unequivocally supported and believed. The first step to solving this problem is to believe survivors before blaming them; very little progress can be made when there is an environment in which rapists are protected and victims villainised. Another solution would be to start education programs for extremely young children that focus on consent – not necessarily in the context of sex, but in talking about bodily autonomy, and once they are older, rape culture. More focus on awareness campaigns such as Bisexual Health Month, which takes place in March, will also generate change. These campaigns are beneficial in helping to spread awareness about how rape disproportionately affects bisexuals.

Sexual assault is an issue affecting all of society, but it is especially important to discuss its nuances in relation to gender when talking about bisexuals. Because bisexuals often date more than one gender, and most sexual assault is done by someone the victim knows,[7] it is important to include unconventional sexual assault in our discussions of this topic in order to help bisexuals. The prevalence of sexual assault for bisexuals is a dire issue that needs to be addressed; the first steps are to rethink how we see it in terms of gender, to stop blaming victims, and to promote understanding by raising awareness.

photographs:
thoughts on self-harm, self-worth, and self-image

by Eleanor Reid

PERSONAL TO-DO LIST at a Teenage Party in 2004:

Make sure not to have eaten all day
Chug 200ml of Tesco value vodka upon arrival
Talk with female friends about how ugly they all think they are
Have three empowering pints together
Take basic white girl selfies with female friends
Get upset and ask friend to delete selfie
Watch as friend posts said selfie online instead
Sit alone while friends are doted on by their male significant others
Give any willing teenage man a blowjob
Run home alone at 3am
Drunkenly self-harm in one or a number of different ways
Block out suicidal thoughts and binge eat

1 – Not Ready for My Close Up

I attended a fee-paying girls' school in a country where education is free, unless your parents choose that it should be otherwise. In other words, it's free unless your parents have the ability to single you out as deserving a little bit better than everyone else. I need not have to add that these people are usually white and rich. I was raised in a working-class environment – it was against all odds that I ended up there. My parents noted early on in my life how 'bookish' I am, and wanted me to make the most of it. I absolutely loved the academic side of my schooling and I know for certain that I'm lucky – I wouldn't be where I am if they hadn't made the decision to send me there.

But there were certain pressures that often pushed me under during the teenage years spent with my classmates, The Girls Who Wanted It All. The friends I'm still in touch with from those years often speak of facing similar struggles, but at the time I (of course) thought it was just me who was unhappy. When I refer to events or scenarios from my secondary school years with people I didn't know back then, they often remark on how wild or crazy it sounds. I had no idea – it was my normality.

For example, one of the main things you had to do when I was a teenage girl was hate yourself. This was an across-the-board, unspoken standard. Accepting a compliment was social suicide. Bulimia was the norm for about one in three; binge eating was for everyone. I've long known that self-esteem and body image are two of the main irritators to my mental health (or lack thereof). Not least in the fact that my favourite way to self-harm remains the first method I ever used – burning myself with a hair straightener – which points us right in the direction of a female grooming ritual as the time of the first incident. Most of the self-harm occurrences during my youth were triggered by photographs or came about in response to seeing other reflections of myself. There were plenty of other self-harmers in my peer group: nothing was ever good enough for The Girls Who Wanted It All.

As a rather tall and unsightly, naturally broad brunette, with a Frida Kahlo-style brow, I found myself in this strangely ruthless world, surrounded by petite, sallow-skinned blondes and lanky porcelain pals with tiny curves and pretty bone structures. This meant that the main fear for me was avoiding being seen as in any way masculine or 'butch'. Butch was bad. A hyper celeb-esque twist on traditional femininity was the goal. This much was made very clear.

Somewhere along the line, the prospect of my appearing as anything other than physically hyper-feminine started to become offensive and upsetting to me. I also started to view the rejected aesthetics of less feminine styles as inherently lesbian. I came to fear being seen as a lesbian more than anything. When I say this, I mean it in a very visual way. I had no morals against same-sex relationships – I just didn't want to *look* like a lesbian (bear with me). I didn't care about how anyone else looked or what anyone else did with their sex lives. I just wanted to be pretty and for boys to like me, because that was one of the main elements of Having It All, right? It sounds so silly and superficial now.

Of course, I was acquainted with absolutely no 'out' lesbians during that time and, furthermore, I had absolutely no idea then that I myself am a bisexual woman. The vibrant array of aesthetics and physical presentations made by lesbian women were unknown to my naïve self in those days, and bisexuality was a word that never even crossed my mind as I unapologetically placed my entire focus on ploughing through life becoming The Girl Who Had It All. My levels of denial are a great source of amusement to me now whenever I visit my teenage bedroom, adorned as it is with photographs of Leonardo DiCaprio and Winona Ryder in almost equal measure – with Ryder probably securing more wall space, if I'm to be completely honest.

II – Painting the Wrong Picture

From my wise perch in 2017, safely away from my destructive teenage lifestyle, I can see that I came about as close as possible (within my personal and physical remits) to becoming The Girl Who Had It All. By the time I was 19, I worked out more times a week than there were days, I had the perfect college boyfriend who worshipped me, I volunteered with half a dozen different charities, I ran my own side project, I had a part-time job and still maintained perfect grades. Yet, sometimes I would find myself in that semi-sleeping state, mumbling 'I want to kill myself' out loud. In a particularly bad meltdown, I lightly overdosed, ripped up or deleted most of the photographs of my preteen years, and deleted all my social media. It wasn't a suicide attempt. I just wanted to fall asleep and for my image to disappear. I never wanted to see my face again when I woke up.

There came a point when I realised that there wasn't much more I could do in life to achieve the goals I had been indoc-trinated to want during my earlier years – I essentially Had It All and I was forced to accept that I no longer knew where else to look for happiness. This resulted in the first time I ever admitted aloud to anyone that I thought I had some sort of chronic depressive disorder. It didn't seem to be intermittent down periods as such; it seemed to be a lingering burden that sometimes was a bit heavier, but always present. I estimate now, though I'm sure it was often obvious to those closest to me, that I suffered in silence for about 8 years before telling my Then-Boyfriend what was up. Though it would be another three years before I was convinced to get any professional help for my Persistent Depressive Disorder, saying it out loud was a turning point for me. He didn't freak out or abandon me like I expected; he was fully supportive and even stated that he respected me all the more for being such a caring person when I felt that way. This particular relationship also allowed me, for the first time, to acknowledge my self-worth in a sexual way. No longer was I drinking too much at teenage parties and basing my self-esteem on giving out blowjobs. I was being respected and loved equally, something that was crucially formative for the person I have now become. I started to think that maybe those girls I grew up with Wanted The Wrong Things.

III – Images of Other People

Around this time, the first season of *Orange Is the New Black* aired on Netflix. I'm not a big TV watcher (which is perhaps one of the reasons I found it difficult to imagine an accurate visual representation of LGBTQ+ women) but this show was recommended to me by a well-trusted source, so I gave it a go. I binge-watched the season with Then-Boyfriend. He stood by, with a great amount of worry in his eyes, as I became entirely fascinated with the beautiful array of different women and the varied portrayals of female sexualities and relationships that I saw on screen. His nervous response to my growing self-acceptance brings up one of the usual prejudices about bisexuality – that bisexuality may equate to promiscuity. Or perhaps, more accurately in this case, that being with a bi woman should emasculate a cisgender straight man. This is all, obviously, untrue and unnecessary, but they are issues I did not then have the knowledge to deescalate or discuss with any great clarity.

Before watching *OITNB*, I had long accepted that I would never be opposed to sleeping with a woman. But I left those thoughts at that level, and didn't think about the fact that such an act would ever have an impact on my sexual identity. This was probably not helped by the fact that I had often witnessed my straight teenage female friends getting drunk and making out for male attention. I never thought about having a relationship with a woman, and I never let it sink in that I could develop feelings for someone who wasn't a man. The show opened my eyes to the many different and very individual ways that LGBTQ+ women can appear; no two fully alike, and all wonderful in their own uniqueness. It also helped me realise that for many years I had been aiming for someone else's physical standard and placing so much of my self-worth in avoiding a stereotype that I shouldn't have worried about at all. On top of this, it finally hit me – I had been living in someone else's dream.

It wasn't until I watched *Orange Is the New Black* that I realised just because I wanted to present myself one way, and not another, didn't mean that I couldn't also be a member of the LGBTQ+ community. The show completely changed how I identified. I went from seeing myself as 'heterosexual but open-minded' to realising 'oh my god, I'm entirely bisexual'. Interestingly, *OITNB* usually gets a lot of criticism for its representation of bisexuality, especially in the character of Piper, but the show was a game-changer for me (and I follow all the actresses on Instagram religiously; sue me).

Looking back, it's clear that I struggled to fit in to hyper-commercialised straight girl expectations (who doesn't?), and I struggled in equal amounts to relate to gay stereotypes. Realising I could be whatever I want, and dress or look however I want, and have it not related in any way to my sexuality was one of the most freeing realisations I've ever had. I had simply not known that that was even an option. The year that followed was one during which I was at my most content, and my self-harm problem was at its most dormant.

IV – Capturing Things Outside a Lens

It's important to note that mental healthcare cannot be approached through a black and white lens. Those of us who fall under a rainbow flag should already be aware of the dangers that accompany viewing the world in black and white. Binaries and stereotypes of any kind are almost always the enemy. Articles, books, films and TV shows (to name just a few mediums) that attempt to deal with mental illnesses almost invariably frustrate me, which is part of the reason I was cautious in writing this essay.

However, no one can ignore the suicide notes of teenagers; the ones we often see floating around tabloid media, stating that they struggled to conform to heteronormative expectations. I've spent a long time trying to determine if my sexuality and my mental illnesses are directly linked. Certainly, it's been said that bisexual people often live with unusually high levels of mental health troubles; it's a claim that has appeared in the majority of LGBTQ+ youth surveys that I've happened across and definitely not the only time it will be mentioned in this book. But it can't exactly be said that all the many self-harm scars on my skin have been caused by some sort of sexual guilt, because I'm aware from living through my own actions that it isn't quite so simple. It can be extremely reductive to speak about mental illnesses in terms of the masses; reducing individuals to numbers and using grand sweeping labels in statement tweets or charity flyers. I know from studying psychology for three years that this is a hurdle for mental health professionals, journalists and activists as well as for patients.

In my case, at least, I think my mental health problems have been aggravated by conservative prejudices and superficial media pressures. That is to say, bisexuality hasn't been a causal factor to my problems; societal frameworks have been the causal factors. I'm now also faced with balancing a very different issue; the fear of telling the world that my life and relationships have changed (as life and relationships are apt to do) and that I now love a woman. I know that this will cause a disturbance for my family and their friends – this is not something I want to cause and it terrifies me.

I am of the opinion that readjusting social norms through writing and gentle open discussion could be one of the best ways to loosen this suffocating framework, and alleviate some of the pressure on those of us with another war already raging in our minds. That said, it requires *so* much bravery to speak up, and sometimes it can even be dangerous to do so.

There are some narrow-minded people we'll never get through to, and there are many LGBTQ+ people who have it much worse than I do. I follow @WhereLoveIsIllegal on Instagram, and I'm regularly overwhelmed by the stories shared on the account – not just because of how unlucky some other LGBTQ+ people are, but because of how *very* lucky I am.

V – A New Frame

'Funny how things change,' my girlfriend once read from a poem, the first time we discussed entering a relationship together – and it is funny. 2015 was the year that I found myself falling hard and fast in love with a woman with whom I thought I was merely striking up a friendship. Even when I realised my feelings for her were much more than that, I assumed anything more was off the cards, so I expected nothing of her. Crushing was hard for a while, but I felt oddly reassured and free in allowing myself to realise, for once, that I knew exactly what I wanted in a partner, and in seeing that it existed out there – outside of frameworks crafted from a social expectation or pressure. I had found an authentic attraction to someone, simply for who she is and nothing else.

Love isn't a cure, of course. I still self-harm sometimes, but never as violently as I once did and usually it's only because it has become a reactionary habit by now. I take medication for the problem and ensure that the situation is monitored by mental health professionals. I still get upset about selfies, I can't use Snapchat, and I go through sprees of untagging pictures on Facebook or deleting images on Instagram. But a lot of my decisions around photographs and images are not self-destructive – they are simply self-protective. More importantly, I now know that the ideas I had of LGBTQ+ (and perhaps also of straight) women were an unnecessary prison of stereotypes that I didn't need to compare myself to. I keep a photograph of my girlfriend and me on my bedside table – and the only thing it makes me to do is smile.

growing up without 'queer'

by Rosy Glen

I COULD HAVE used the term 'queer' when I was growing up. Fifteen-year-old me had no idea that twenty-seven-year-old me would have found a term that finally fit; socially, sexually and culturally.

I'm lucky enough to come from a generation that loves to reclaim. Some of us emblazon ourselves with 'fag' and 'dyke', perhaps because parts of society have told us that our identities are something to be ashamed of and we've decided to wear them with pride as one big, fat 'fuck you'.

We want to reclaim and divert the power of such strong words. Words that ring from the aggressor's mouths, angry and guttural. Snarled. The French *gouine* (dyke) has a much angrier vibe than *lesbienne*. If that anger is going to exist, I want that anger to be mine, to be ours. And a part of me likes to believe that if I use it myself then I'm anticipating it to hurt less when other people decide to use it against me. We anticipate the historical sting and we decide that if there's going to be pain it'll be on our terms.

But I'm sure we horrify our elders; they must mutter about us, flinching at our word choices. It's probable that some of them were the ones who suffered those words firsthand. 'Queer' used to be a slur, lips curled as it was hurled overarm into the crowd or subtly, softly and under breath, side-eye while slinking by.

Because I came out circa 2005, I was lucky enough to bypass 'queer' as an insult and was instead thrown headfirst into a pejorative 'gay'. (That one lasted for years, right up until my early university days. I remember feeling shock that grown adults were still showing their disapproval through 'that's so gay'.) Language stings, but luckily it evolves, and I would say that 'queer' has been reclaimed and is now a celebration. It is an umbrella term, embodying everything LGBTQ+ and yet, for me, it can also simply mean 'not-heterosexual'. But I haven't always had this solid reassurance that sexuality isn't black and white. I didn't quite know what I was coming out as when I was younger, and I would have appreciated some gentle reassurance that sexual fluidity isn't a negative.

During periods of strongly identifying as a lesbian and having long-term relationships with women, I found a comfortable nook that I'd happily settle into – until out of the woodwork would creep an unsettling attraction to men that I have never been able to properly explain. Until very recently, my life has been peppered with mild frenzies of 'Here we go again, I'm sleeping with men and I don't know how to define myself'. I've had periods of feeling not quite at home with either of the defining terms I was offered ('bisexual' or 'lesbian'), feeling like a fraud, feeling as if I owed people an explanation if I were to be seen as valid in this minefield of sexuality. Validity cropped up quite a lot: valid using the term 'lesbian' on the days I loved women but still found myself attracted to men; valid using 'bisexual' on the days I found men attractive but knew I could never commit to a relationship with one; valid on the days I hated all the terms and wanted to loosen the restrictions that language, society, and overall myself, were placing upon me.

I love 'queer' for its ambiguity, creativity and individuality. I love the freedom it allows me and all it has offered me in terms of inclusivity and access to a community. My 'queer' means I am not heterosexual; it means that physically, I'm attracted to a huge mix of people; it means that, for now, it's women I fall in love with. It gives me hope for shifts in gender binaries, for the concepts of masculinity and femininity to exist in new, better and less toxic ways.

'Queer' gives me hope for a world that's not afraid of evolving. 'Queer', for me, illustrates the bold and the beautiful of my sexuality, giving me freedom and community, and above all, reassurance that I am valid.

stuck in the middle:
being bi and non-binary

by Robert O'Sullivan

I'VE ONLY EVER come out as bi to one person, and I remember it vividly. A few years previously I had told my parents that I was no longer Catholic, and was now some form of agnostic – I endured the various 'fence-sitter' jokes for years, which made me extremely hesitant to come out again, this time about my sexuality. Yet, I did: we were in the car, driving up a tree-lined country road, my college LGBT Society hoodie stuffed into my bag. I'm still not sure why, but I just had this feeling, deep down, that I had to say something. So I did. I remember those words exactly: 'Mam, I'm bi. It might mean nothing's different in the end, it might make a difference. I don't know, but I just had to tell you'. And nothing more was said, really, at least not on that matter. And over time, unlike my religious reveal years before, there hasn't been much mentioned on the subject, other than random awkward questions when going on a night out: 'Who are you going with? Is it a boy or a girl?' It was never usually a date, so it really didn't matter, but it was awkward. The experience with my parents coloured my attitudes on my life and ideas of 'coming out'. 'I would do it a bit more "punk rock",' I told myself, 'a bit DIY. If anyone asks, or anyone finds out, I'll act cool and answer calmly, as if it's no big deal. Because it's no big deal, right?' Then I had a reve-lation about my gender, too, and gender identity as a whole.

When people find out you identify as something other than male or female, one of the first few (very well-meaning) questions is something like 'Well, how did you know you wer-en't male?' to which there really isn't an answer. It's just a... feeling. I always felt differently, and then one day I heard the terms 'genderqueer' *(someone who identifies as neither, both or a combination of male and female)* and 'genderfluid' *(someone whose gender identity is dynamic, and may change from day-to-day, moment-to-moment)* and something just clicked. Later, in university, I came out to someone as non-binary. Or genderqueer. I can't remember which word I used at the time – probably genderqueer. And while, for a year or so, I was as tentative to come out as I had been before, I eventu-ally embraced the same philosophy of 'Eh, fuck it' as I had when I came out as bi. Quite like being bi, being non-binary comes with its own set of problematic issues. Pronouns are a big part of it: a lot of non-binary people go with the gender neutral classic they/them; some go with something like xie or xer. That 'Eh, fuck it' streak again reared its head, as I eventu-ally decided that any and all pronouns work for me.

Preconceptions go beyond language and feelings. People presume you should be – no, you *have* to be – some David Bowie/Tilda Swinton-esque paragon of androgyny. For one, I was never quite svelte enough to pull-off the 'Thin White

Duke' look, but it's crucial to remember that gender presentation is not gender identity – a concept trans people have to combat, and one cisgender people *(people who identify with the gender they were assigned at birth)* don't understand. I remember once coming out to a large room of people, while on stage, and was met with looks of pure incredulity. Months later someone in the crowd told me that they thought I was 'spoofing' because *'Come on, you're a big beardy dude'*. To be fair to those people, I get it: it's not exactly the norm. And hey, that wasn't a queer space, so why should they know? The naive 'baby gay' that I was went into various LGBTQ+ spaces expecting them to get it a bit more, but it wasn't much better.

When I write about queer spaces or groups it tends to be negative, mainly because the bad experiences I've had have been very bad. It's not all terrible; the first person I came out to as non-binary/genderqueer was a fantastic bi woman, who was so supportive when I needed someone. But overall, the LGBTQ+ community was not as welcoming or knowledgeable as I would've hoped about the intricacies of identities outside of L and G (but mainly G). I first showed up and said nothing about my actual identities and orientations, so it was presumed I was a gay man. The most pervasive questions had to do with sex: what was my type, was I a top or a bottom, what was my number etc., all questions I was terribly uncomfortable with. Eventually I let it be known that I was bi, and the same 'fence-sitter' and 'pick a side' jokes I had heard as an irreligious child were made anew. And they still weren't funny. 'Being bi,' I was told, 'is just a stepping stone to being gay,' as if the person telling me this was the Michael Collins of queerness. Eventually, as I did before, I learned to brush these jokes and barbs off, but when I told people I was non-binary? Oh my. 'You can't be bi and non-binary! Bi means two!' I was repeatedly told that my identity was wrong, that it couldn't be real, or true, or that I was just incredibly confused. And despite their previous ineptitude at being a gentle guiding hand in the subtle world of queer identity, I believed them. I doubted myself, and began to hate myself.

This is a debate that still goes on in LGBTQ+ circles today: is it transphobic to be bi? The mere existence of an identity of 'pansexual' would suggest that it is, right? If bi means both or two, or if bisexual specifically means being attracted to both men and women, then surely that's an exclusionary term that we should be phasing out of our communal lexicon? Another separate but related issue, one would think, is the problem with profiles on dating apps like Grindr listing preferences based on race – that is undoubtedly problematic, so surely a term that excludes a whole group of people based on identifying as *some third option* is a similar type of awful? Well, partly, *yes*: I'm sure some bisexual people will not date non-binary people, the same way some lesbians won't date bi women, but the term itself isn't inherently transphobic. Many bisexual people, myself included, think of the 'bi' as meaning attraction to 'two or more genders' or being attracted to 'the same gender as yourself, and others'. Even using its most reductive definition, to mean just two genders, who's to say that those two must be male and female?

Despite the work of plenty of bisexual and non-binary activists and educators to correct the general misconception, this 'debate' rages on. For years I had people lecture me about this, about my own identity. And for a while, I believed them: I identified as pansexual, even though that label (a perfectly fine, wonderful label at that) never really felt right; I started to shave my face and paint my nails to try to match up as best I could with that common stereotype of someone neither male nor female. It took me a long, long time to come back to that weird 'punk-rock' way of thinking: that labels and identities are for you to define yourself, not for some random person with a backwards understanding of Latin root words to dictate to you. People can try to tell you that your terms don't make sense, or make tired jokes about sitting on fences to passive-aggressively bring you down, or insist you should have to fit a prescribed mould of outward presentation to be believable, but *fuck them*, I know who I am. I am a bearded bisexual non-binary bastard, and there's nothing wrong or hypocritical about that.

california here i come:
how the o.c. helped me understand my bisexual idenity

by Lauren Vevers

I WAS A shy teenager with a handful of bookish friends, but when I turned 14 I latched onto a girl who was very different to me. She loved talking about boys and make-up and the kind of lives we'd have as adults, all things I hadn't contemplated at that age. Her defining feature was her long blonde hair, which she'd spend hours straightening until it laid flat down her back in a silvery wave. Our friendship was built around MSN messenger conversations and popular TV. In 2004, that was *The O.C.*

The O.C. is an American teen drama series created by Josh Schwartz that first aired in the UK on Channel 4. It follows the story of brooding teen Ryan Atwood as he's adopted by a wealthy family in Newport Beach. His step-brother Seth is nerdy and verbose with a hopeless crush on popular girl Summer. Ryan is attracted to Marissa, Summer's best friend, who is as troubled as she is beautiful and just happens to live next door. The improbability of it all is part of its appeal. Growing up in a small city in the northeast corner of England, the golden sands of California felt far away. Anything was possible in Orange County.

'Do you fancy Seth or Ryan more?' my new friend would ask over and over. I always picked Ryan because it seemed to be what she wanted me to say. After school I would go to her house. She had an older brother who liked to play *Grand Theft Auto* and say very little. I observed him from a distance with the curiosity of a wildlife photographer. I was fascinated by the size of his hands, the length of his limbs. I wondered if I was attracted to him. I couldn't be sure.

By the time the second season of *The O.C.* came around our friendship had waxed and waned. I'd grown bored of the same conversations, although I was content in our after-school routine. One evening her mother decided to give me a make-over in what I can only assume she thought was a gesture of kindness. 'We'll make you look nice for the boys,' she said. She covered my face in powder, drew lines around my lips. When she finished, my skin was heavy and tight. My friend and I sat on the sofa while her brother and his friends sipped beers. When they showed no interest in my transformation, I was disappointed. Her mother was sympathetic. 'Oh well, never mind,' she said. It wasn't as simple as feeling rejected, there were other emotions too. Shyness, discomfort, confusion. I was beginning to learn about the rituals associated with attraction, and within that, trying to unpick my own desires. I fancied boys, probably. Yet something was missing.

We only watched a handful of episodes of *The O.C.* together after that. For a short while, the male protagonists take a backseat. In the episode 'The New Kids On The Block' we're introduced to Alex. She works in a club called The Bait Shop, has a butterfly tattoo on her upper arm, and is attracted to both men and women. Later in the series, her earnest friendship with Marissa begins to show signs of something more. In 'The Lonely Hearts Club', they go on a spontaneous date to the beach. 'The tide's turned,' Alex says before they lean in and kiss. A lot of things made sense to me then. My friend turned the TV off, unmoved. I wanted to tell her what was going through my head, but I couldn't articulate it. Even if I'd been able to, I was plagued by the fear that she'd think I fancied her, that I'd get ridiculed because of it. I never went back to her house and instead retreated into myself, having discovered the flicker of something I wouldn't fully embrace until my early twenties – that maybe I was like Alex.

I began to seek out representations of bisexuality in TV and film. Aside from Alex and Marissa, I found two on-screen kisses between women: Kathryn and Cecile in the film *Cruel Intentions* (1999), and Madonna and Britney at the VMAS in 2003. This was disheartening. That *O.C.* storyline had opened the door to new possibilities, but I felt it closing again before I had the chance to walk through. I'd never met anyone who was openly gay, let alone bisexual. We weren't taught about sexuality in sex ed, just about the mechanics of intercourse between cisgender men and cisgender women. As a teenager, pop culture served as a kind of framework by which I lived my life, so to find there was no one I could identify with was difficult. Why wasn't anyone talking about bisexuality? It was as though it didn't exist.

I missed the cultural phenomenon of *Buffy The Vampire Slayer* when it first appeared in 1997. It was praised for its depiction of a gay relationship and the first lesbian sex scene broadcast on network TV – however, its erasure of bisexuality in the character of Willow is equally worth noting. Willow is studious and reserved, her ability to hack computers integral to the advancement of the plot. Early in the show she falls for Oz, a high school senior and werewolf, who remains her romantic interest for several series. When they break up, Willow meets Tara at a campus Wicca gathering and eventually they enter into a relationship. From this point, her character is reframed as a lesbian. Whilst I respect the importance of self-identifying – and Willow does call herself a lesbian in the show – the writers behind this fictional world have simplified her sexuality. Their message is: if you're a woman dating a man you're heterosexual, while if you're a woman dating a woman you're a lesbian. These are the same lazy assumptions that are at large today, and I think they're at work here, affecting the writers' mindset and moving them to erase the possibility of bisexuality. Whilst it might not seem immediately damaging, lack of representation in media perpetuates the real-life stereotype that bisexual people must either be straight or gay, or similarly, that bisexuality is only a symptom of greed or indecisiveness. The use of binary categories erases the experience of those who fall outside them.

Looking back, watching *The O.C.* was formative for me. It planted a seed, showed me an alternative way to be. Still, bi representation is not uncomplicated. Bisexual characters are frequently portrayed as deviants, their sexuality nearly always a manifestation of a dark or mysterious past. Alex is no exception. Expelled from high school, her reputation as a 'bad girl' is reflected in her physical appearance, which is strikingly different from that of her peers. She is an outsider, an other. Jenny Scheuteur from *The L Word* (2004 – 2009) is another example of a character which fits this trope. From the outset she displays narcisstic tendancies and a selfish egotism that makes it difficult for viewers to identify with her. The 'depraved bisexual' is hypersexual, manipulative and unstable. Especially in later seasons, Jenny embodies many of these traits. Once more in season 1, having broken up with her boyfriend Tim, she tells an old friend 'I think I'm bisexual'. Despite this, her bisexuality is gradually erased over the course of the show and by season 4, she identifies as a lesbian. Alice Pieseki, the other openly bisexual character on *The L Word,* is continually mocked by her lesbian peers for her sexual preference, perpetuating the notion that bisexual people simply can't make up their minds. Even in *The L Word,* which is deemed to be relatively progressive within the LGBTQ+ community, bisexuality only gets a cursory look in. For the most part, Jenny's and Alice's relationships are with women and overall, the narrative hinges on lesbian relationships. Whilst this in itself isn't neccesarily a problem, in the wider context of a TV show that is meant to be inclusive, bisexuality is once again erased.

Technology has made it easier for teenagers to connect with each other, to have more conversations and to build communities. Representations of bisexuality in TV are increasing and according to some statistics, 28% of all recurring LGBTQ+ characters are bisexual.[1] But in the past decade, despite the Internet's growing reach, I haven't personally noticed much difference in the way bisexuality is represented. Teenagers are sponges; they soak in the world around them. They're smart, impressionable, funny, confused, and should be offered support to help them transition into adulthood. Adolesence is hard enough without feeling invisible, so for this reason, I think there needs to be a cultural shift towards positive bi representation in television aimed at a teenage audience. This means more convincing, visible bisexual characters, drama written and produced by bisexual people, and writing that reflects a breadth of bisexual experience, especially from BAME voices. Whilst I can see there are glimmers of hope in the move towards positive bi representation, like the Amazon series *Transparent* (2014 -) for instance, there's some way to go. Until damaging attitudes which support real-life bisexual stereotypes change, it's unlikely the entertainment industry will change either.

As an experiment, I re-watched *The O.C.* The writing is clunky and the teenagers are implausibly mature for their age. Most irksome is the way the development of Alex and Marissa's relationship is used as a device to service the more prevalent love story between Ryan and Marissa. Before the end of the series, Alex's character leaves Newport Beach and doesn't return. It took me a long time to come to terms with my bisexuality, and half the battle was accepting that I could retain my own identity regardless of the gender of my partner. *The O.C.*, whilst imperfect, gave me a tiny spark of empowerment. Still, by the time it came to an end, my friendship with the girl from school had fizzled out. In sixth form we barely spoke. There were many reasons why we no longer hung out together, not least that relationships between teenage girls are often fickle. However, if I could've found the language to articulate my bisexuality, or even if there was a space in which I could discuss my sexuality freely without judgement, there's a chance we'd have stayed friends. Our experiences of watching the show were vastly different, and with no way to bridge the gap in understanding between us, maybe it was inevitable that our relationship broke down. Bi-erasure, as well as existing in a broad cultural sense, also has a personal impact on the individual. In my case, bi-erasure made it difficult for my teenage self to express an important aspect of my identity. If I'd been able to look to popular culture for more examples of bisexuality, I certainly would have felt less alone.

defining terms:
how i finally started listening to my brain and body

by Kathryn Lesko

AS A CHILD, I was lucky because I got to grow up in the San Francisco Bay Area. A place which earned the nickname 'gay capital of the world' in the 1960s, it has maintained a high level of LGBTQ+ activism and social support since then. This means that most kids in my community grew up talking about and interacting with a very open LGBTQ+ community. Intellectually, I knew from a young age that lots of people had non-heterosexual romantic feelings; I had close friends with gay parents, though no close queer peers until high school (that I knew of at the time). Different sexualities were part of normal life, nothing to get excited about. *Intellectually* that made sense to me, on a theoretical level that did not seep into my skin.

I first recall being conscious of feelings for other girls at roughly the age of 11. I acted mostly like a socially acceptable straight girl growing up – I may have been 'allergic to pink' and tended to avoid dresses, but I still played with horses and had a Magic Attic doll. But one night I was at a slumber party with my three best friends from elementary school, and we were making pacts and talking about the future. One friend wanted assurance that none of us would end up being lesbian. We all agreed, but I distinctly remember feeling disappointed when they all so easily assured her it wouldn't be a problem. I didn't have any other little baby queers to talk to, though, and we girls only ever shared our crushes on guys, so any feelings I had for my gal friends got pushed into a tiny box in my head labelled 'not applicable', and I moved on. Flash forward a few years to high school. I had by this point had a 'boyfriend', and plenty of guy crushes. I was pretty sure I was a 'normal' girl. All those weird puberty feelings were still tucked into the 'not applicable' box, forlorn and forgotten.

You have to understand I am a very stubborn person. It's something I take pride in: I fix my sights on a goal, and damnit, I will reach it come hell or high water – usually regardless of physical and/or mental health. Did I mention this trait also comes with a strong dose of self-esteem issues and a tendency to hold myself to the highest standard I can find, with no ability to recognise when enough is enough? No? Well, it does. I assume I am always inferior, never doing enough. Partially because of this, I draw a lot of happiness and ego from making those around me happy. This applies to my friends, my colleagues, and most especially to my relationships. Because I have never seen myself as an attractive person, I assume I'm the reacher, and I do everything in my power to make my partner happy, regardless (to a degree) of how it makes me feel. *So* we've got a problematic personal image issue, a tendency towards intense emotional connection, and an internal closet nailed so tightly shut the nails are soldered into knots on the inside. And we're entering high school.

Mature, educated Kat speaking: The difficulty with a coming out story from a chronological standpoint is that we now have words to describe concepts I could not have begun to grasp as a young person. So, before we move forward let me tell you a little bit about Gender Theory, and just how difficult it is to realise and understand same-sex attraction in a heteronormative world. Especially when you still have emotional and kind-of heterosexual physical attraction. It is so easy to ignore the little voice in your head going 'Oh, but that girl is pretty! Why not go flirt with her?' when there's another voice talking louder (because it's been given more agency) and identifying easier, much less terrifying targets. Go read a couple of papers on the Theory of Gender and Power, and the Minority Stress Framework.[1,2]

And now back to high school.

I loved theatre, and dance, and music, and science, and English, and Spanish and... yeah, you got it. I was that annoying kid who loves *everything* she can get her mind into. This included a senior we'll call First Love. We fell hard and fast at the end of my freshman year (his senior year). We had a summer, then he went off to college in Massachusetts. We were together for three years. Gods, I loved him so much. Sex? Wasn't really a thing. Partially because I was young, partially because of the distance, partially because I hadn't wrapped my head around the whole penis thing. The weird bit about sexual attraction, at least how I've experienced it, is that the pre-coital lust feels the same regardless of the gender of the person I'm with. It's the act where I have a road-block. But there's some hard-wired biology in there telling you (through hormones talking to your hypothalamus) that the penis will make you feel good. So you keep trying, because your brain (and society) is telling you that's what you're supposed to do. Over and over and over.

Eventually, First Love and I broke up because of distance, and I was feeling like I needed to explore myself before I left high school. There was this magical creature in my class we'll call Edward *(he didn't come out as trans until college, so while I use male pronouns, he was female-presenting in high school)* who seemed to want me as a toy, and I willingly let that happen. Make-out sessions in public at the school dances? Check. At the school Snow Trip on his hotel bed? Check. Discussion about queerness and feelings and whatnot? Completely avoided and ignored. My memory is (once again the inferiority complex talking) that he couldn't possibly have actually liked me, that I was his plaything, and that that was okay with me. We've never talked about it, so I have no idea how he really felt then, but that was what my brain was telling me. In any case, partially due to that relationship with a female-presenting person, I graduated high school identifying as bisexual. This word seemed to fit with how I operated in the world, so I accepted it, became it, and presented it.

I went away to college telling myself I was *not* going to date boys anymore. Every sexual interaction I'd had with boys up until then had felt like it was missing something, thought I couldn't identify at the time what exactly that was. I was going to steer clear of the male arena entirely, if only to give myself the chance to explore the female side of my interests. But two months in I found an amazing man we'll call Jake, and we dated for – surprise – 6 years. For a while, everything seemed good. Was I faking orgasm the majority of the times we had penetrative intercourse? Yes. Did I tell myself that this was normal, that I was fulfilled by our emotional connection and that I didn't need the physical part? Of course. Did he seem sexually appeased? As far as I could tell I was doing my job in that department, so why change anything? Though at that time I was 'out' to the world, I'm not convinced I was really out to myself. That box labelled 'not applicable' was still buried deep in my head. It took some long, drunken conversations with my amazing (and very straight) girl friends to accept that I shouldn't still be faking orgasms 5 years into a relationship that could very easily and naturally have ended in marriage. That made me think pretty hard. Maybe I *wasn't* physically attracted to him. All these straight girls really seemed to enjoy sex and penises and all the things that come with it. I knew that wasn't my thing, but I did love him. Wasn't that proof that I was at least bi? I ended up making a vow to myself that I would stop faking it during sex. I *immediately* lost any inclination to interact with him in that way. The minute I was in this thing for me, not for him, all my reactions changed. I avoided, I stopped asking, and eventually he stopped asking. We were living together and it was a pretty stressful year, so we chalked a lot of our issues up to stress.

About six months after we'd stopped having sex, I started a very scary late-night conversation. I said the words 'I think I'm gay'. Using that word really changed how I thought about the situation and myself. 'Bisexual' always felt like I still belonged at least somewhat to the heteronormative world *(though statistically this is very much not true – there are a number of papers identifying the bi population as the most marginalised because they don't fit in anywhere and are criticised by both heterosexual and homosexual groups[3])*. 'Gay' meant I was setting myself apart from every lie I'd told myself growing up. It meant I didn't want to have my life story end with me and a guy and our kids. It meant that I needed to start a whole new plan, which was terrifying, especially for someone as detail-oriented as I am. But finally, it felt like I was taking myself into account, and that seemed more important than the fear of what the future would hold.

So we talked. We talked and I cried and he went back inside his shell that I'd spent years breaking down, and I cried some more. I cried myself to sleep for weeks. I had a very hard time explaining how I was a lesbian who fell in love with men. This was my pattern, and those feelings were never not true. But I was clearly, at least *functionally*, gay. Was I actually trans? I asked myself. But I have some very close trans friends and body dysmorphia was never something I'd experienced. I was in the right body to match my identity; it was my sexuality that didn't match, that was *wrong*.

Here's the weird bit: coming to terms with internalised homophobia. The hatred I felt for myself and my identity had absolutely *nothing* to do with the outside world. I love my gay friends and we will fight together to make this world an equal, accepting place. But inside? I was angry with myself for *failing* those life goal images I'd set out for myself. I'd secretly always planned to *blend in*, to cope with my weird socially unaccept-able feelings by siphoning them into my 'not applicable' box for the rest of my life. Keep in mind, by that point I was 23 years old. I had graduated college with far too many honours, I lived in a studio apartment with my boyfriend of six years, I had a solid job in a field I cared about. *I was doing everything right*, according to society. Was I going to just throw this all away to have orgasms with my partner? After a while, I real-ised the answer was going to be Yes.

So, like any good baby lesbian, I started watching *The L Word*. The beauty of *The L Word* is that it gives us non-heterosexual, women-loving creatures some sort of expectation to set up. I could begin building my life-goal images again, altering them to fit this new identity. I didn't have any close real-life examples of what that looked like, but I could imagine based on the show. At that time it was *the only* reliable, commercially available imagery for what a functional lesbian relationship looked like. Okay, I thought. I can do this. I accepted a Master's degree program at a prestigious east coast school and moved across the country. Jake and I broke up as I packed the U-haul for good. *I still loved him.* That bit I still had no explanation for. *But* I was building this new box in my head with more space and lots of memories, also labelled 'not applicable'. This time, I dumped all my previous relationships into it. I was a Lesbian with a capital L. I wasn't a Gold Star Lesbian, but that's okay; those are rare (hence the gold star). But the deep-seated feelings that went with those relationships? Into the box, seal the lid.

I actively spent my year on the east coast avoiding relationships and working on my mental image of myself. I immediately joined the climbing gym and vowed to make it my only hobby. My French horn stayed in her case. I didn't audition for orchestra, or any dance troupes, and I avoided theatre like the plague. I was going to get good grades and make myself hot for all the lesbians I needed to attract. Let's be clear: at this point I had spent an entire year becoming a gym rat, gaining all kinds of fun muscle and losing a lot of the pudge I'd acquired over the years. Yet, I still saw myself as an unattractive, awkward blob. *And I still had crushes on guys.* What the fuck, brain? I thought. I'm gay now! I've figured it out! I've solved all the puzzles! I'm acknowledging the pretty ladies and considering flirting with them, so why do I still notice the boys? In essence, I ripped open my not applicable box and dumped it on the floor, asking 'Is there a better way to organise this? Am I missing something?'.

I visited the northeast this spring and had a long talk with my Very Wise Queer Friend Ben, and they had a fancy new, deconstructed term that described my entire life and removed all the 'not applicable' boxes: *Pan*romantic, *Homo*sexual. Though there is much debate about Pan and Bi prefixes, I use Pan- to indicate a lack of differentiation among gender presentations. Basically, I don't find one gender presentation (male, female, femme, non-binary, etc.) to be necessarily more romantically attractive than another. I do, however, find myself only having lasting sexual feelings for female-presenting identities. Thus, by separating the two pieces of a relationship with another human, I can fit myself nicely into an identity that feels right. Everything suddenly makes sense. I can come to terms with, and accept, all of the *feelings* I've had, because feelings are allowed now. The terms I can use to talk about myself include feelings but not sex with guys. Can I use this on forms and checked boxes? Not yet, and probably not for a very long time. But at least I can begin to use it when I talk to people who ask, and when I try to explain myself to myself. How do I work with this in real life? I have no idea. Will I still need these boxes and categories once I've really become comfortable with myself and stop needing a group to identify with? Maybe... but maybe not. Ask me again in a year or two. But I think I've finally managed to hit the Self-Acceptance button, right before turning 25. It feels amazing.

'not like that, like this':
bisexuality, sex, and chronic illness

by Alice T

MY EX-GIRLFRIEND AND I had a joke that we loved, that we saved up to use on unsuspecting idiots who asked 'that question'. We'd look them in the eye, assume a highly unlikely physical pose, gesture to ourselves and laugh: 'this is how lesbians have sex'. Because that is what people want to know, isn't it? How two women share intimacy. It didn't matter that I was bisexual, or that sex and sexuality are complicated. It all boiled down to that ever-mysterious, behind-closed-doors, soft-focus moment. It all came down to fucking.

It was my first relationship with another woman, and I loved the powerful feeling it gave me. I had penetrated the mystery, I was a proper queer person, now, because I was having queer sex. I'd gained membership to a secret club, a club people asked questions about, and now I could look sage and give advice. Of course, it never occurred to me to stop and ask questions. What was queer sex? What did that mean? Was I happy? All I could do was bask in that rosy, new-love glow, and allude to this glamorous, wonderful world I had now entered. And it was wonderful. We were both supposed to be doing masters degrees, and in those first months, very, very little got done. We did work out, however, where it was best to have sex in the University Library. The big, cool building was a warren of passageways and spiral stairs, and nobody ever came into the Early European History stacks. Except us. A delicious secret, smelling of sunshine and old books.

Around the same time, my vulva began to hurt. At the beginning, I thought I'd been scratched 'down there' by a hang-nail. It stung, but that had happened before. That's what happened, I thought, a risk of the territory. Queer sex begetting queer injury, the sort you can't talk about in polite company. On the phone, I regaled my friend with news of my 'sex injury'. As if a sore vulva were handcuff bruises or spanking marks, I was proud of it. But the scratch didn't heal. Instead, it ran from a sharp pain to a dull, throbbing ache. Over the next six or seven weeks, it became steadily more difficult to walk, or to cycle, or to sit comfortably for very long. Eventually, I was left sleepless and in agony, sent back and forth by the local A&E department. They weren't unsympathetic, just baffled. Eventually, in desperation, tired of me turning up crying in the middle of the night, they referred me to a gynaecological dermatologist. Out of interest, there aren't very many of those. Dermatological gynaecology is the unfashionable end of the vagina business – there is no pregnancy, no babies, no glory of a safe delivery. The gynaecologist, who I vaguely remember was nice, and young, took less than five minutes to diagnose me. 'A textbook case,' she said. A textbook case of Lichen Sclerosus.

You probably haven't heard of LS. I am sorry, if you have, because that probably means that you, or someone you know, suffers from it. It is a chronic, relapsing and remitting skin condition that primarily affects the genital skin, most usually the mucus membrane of the vulva of women. Lichen Sclerosus is an autoimmune condition, not contracted through or affected by earlier sexual activity. It can affect anyone, at any age, although it is uncommon in menstruating women.

That's a lot of information, really, to take in. Basically, in cis women and girls, Lichen Sclerosus tends to affect the vulva (the skin around the entrance to the vagina) and the skin around the anus (back passage). The vulva changes, and shrinks. This can make penetration impossible, and in some cases, orgasm becomes impossible when the clitoris disappears. The bad news about all of this is that it is a lifelong condition, rather than an illness. Because it primarily affects post-menopausal women, it is usually considered a chronic illness of later life, but it can affect women of any age. The good news is that there are simple, effective treatments which, in most cases, lead to remission. The treatment is a topical steroid, which suppresses the immune response in the body, and stops your body attacking the vulval skin.

After my diagnosis and treatment, our sex life changed. I couldn't have sex the way I usually did, couldn't be penetrated, often couldn't orgasm. Especially in the early days of the illness, I was often in far too much pain to even imagine having sex. There was another side effect: the steroids meant that I gained weight. So, not only was I in pain, but my body was changing in ways I couldn't control. I could feel, throughout this process, the heavy weight of my girlfriend's disappointment. However, I needed the treatment, needed to get better: there was nothing I could do.

At the time that all of this was going on, I was twenty-one. I didn't know then what I know now, about sex, and how it can change, evolve and grow. I didn't know how to ask for what I wanted. I didn't realise that I had as much right to be having a good time, to be safe, and happy, as everyone else. I thought, essentially, that my right to a good sex life was already in jeopardy: I was bisexual. I was already a shadow-creature, living between the worlds of 'straight' and 'gay' sex, whatever that meant. I presumed that any kind of sex life at all ended upon diagnosis with a chronic illness.

The doctors did nothing to dispel this myth: most of them told me how difficult my predicament was, and how unusual. No useful information was given about sex or how to have it, let alone queer sex. Sex, it was implied, was off the table for me for the rest of my life. Dutifully, I relayed this information back to my girlfriend. It sat on the table between us, slowly growing, until eventually it obscured our view of each other. After I told her, we never had sex again. I felt that I had killed something accidentally, like breaking the stem off a plant. We never spoke about sex, never tried, never so much as kissed after that. There was no broaching the subject. Two long, platonic years later, we broke up.

It wasn't surprising to me that the medical staff who I frequently saw weren't able to help with questions about sex, and especially about queer sex. After all, it was a joke, wasn't it? A question to which nobody knew the answer. A party trick: 'this is how lesbians have sex'. Except that I wasn't even a lesbian, and I certainly wasn't sure how to have sex again. I was a bisexual woman with a strange illness, steroidal weight gain, and chronic pain. Nobody knew what do to with me.

But this isn't actually a hopeless story. Most of us grow into our sexual identities gradually, during our teenage years, led by gut feeling, minimal education, and peer pressure. I had been taught things, shown things in bedrooms at house parties, figured things out using the dial-up internet in my parent's house, desperate not to be discovered. At twenty-one, I was given the unusual opportunity to reshape and redesign my sexual identity, from the bottom up. I felt lost, of course, but hopeful. Not only was I going to have sex again, comfortable, pleasurable sex; I was going to learn as much about sex and sexuality as I possibly could.

The world of sex education, revisited as an adult, is absolutely fascinating. It is also largely horrifying. For example, in 26 US states, abstinence is required to be emphasised as part of school sex education.[1] And that is just education pertaining to heterosexual sex and sexuality. Eight states in the US prohibit entirely the teaching of homosexuality, with at least two states legally requiring that homosexuality be portrayed negatively, in relation to HIV.[2] In the UK, Section 28, designed to stop schools teaching pupils about homosexuality, stipulated that they should 'not intentionally promote homosexuality or publish material with the intention of promoting homosexuality' or 'promote the teaching in any maintained school of the acceptability of homosexuality as a pretended family relationship'.[3] This was only repealed in 2000, too late for me: my sex education contained very little information about even heterosexual sex and sexuality, and this was a common experience amongst my peers. Mostly, it was an introduction to human reproduction, in biological terms, and a day of being separated by perceived gender and taught about menstruation. Children and young teenagers are not adequately prepared to encounter their own bodies, let alone other peoples' – it is not unsurprising that when faced with a crisis in sex or sexuality, people suddenly realise how little they actually know.

There are, however, so many people and organisations doing excellent work around sex and sexuality, and when I took my first nervous steps towards re-educating myself about intimacy and pleasure, I was delighted to find such brilliant resources. I wanted, in particular, information about queer sex, or sex as a queer person. Or, I suppose, more broadly, any sex that wasn't 'penis-in-vagina' sex, traditionally perceived as 'straight'. There is an extensive and ongoing debate about whether or not, as a bisexual person, you inhabit a 'straight' relationship when you are dating a person of the opposite sex, or whether you, by dint of being bisexual, queer that relationship. I do not have the answer, but I did know that however my future partners might define their gender, the sex we would be having would be traditionally considered queer.

The first port of call was, perhaps because I am a millennial, YouTube. Sex education on this platform is largely unregulated, and alongside the good stuff, I also found plenty of non-intersectional feminism, transphobia, biphobia, and straightforward misinformation: enter at your own risk. Perhaps the best resource I discovered was Dr Lindsey Doe's channel *Sexplanations*. The channel is under the umbrella of educational entertainment channels produced by brothers Hank and John Green. These aim to offer curriculum-standard educational videos on a wide range of topics, from algebra to ancient history. The *Sexplanations* channel is an outlier, as it is not incorporated into curriculum, but it aims to be educational and shame-free. Doe is a doctor of human sexuality, and the channel covers everything from masturbation to safe anal sex, from pregnancy to trans health. Watching the channel, I realised I was not only learning a huge amount, but I was altering the way I thought about sex entirely. Freed from shame or an agenda other than education, the channel dealt frankly and joyfully with the messy, curious, untaught aspects of sexuality. Perhaps most vitally, Dr Doe's channel introduced me to ideas of consent which went far beyond what I had previously understood consent to contain. Most useful was her 'Will/Want/Won't' list.

This idea is extremely simple: in three columns, list every act associated with sex that you can imagine, and categorise it by the three preferences. This allows you to understand your preferences, as well as things you might be new to, but wish to try. I have used this technique with subsequent partners before intimacy and it has been an excellent ice-breaker, allowing both of us to frankly discuss what we do and don't like in bed. It's also a good way for me to bring up my illness: if a partner requires regular penetrative sex for them to feel comfortable in a relationship, for example, this issue can be raised early. It sometimes feels a little clinical, disrupts the drunk rush for the bedroom, the giddiness of that first undressing. For me, however, the exchange is worth it. There are, in fact, bonuses: in reading other peoples' lists, I learn about things I have never thought about, and get to try them. It decentres my illness, allowing it to be discussed alongside restraints or fancy underwear, giving it a lesser significance, which makes me feel more comfortable.

Another really brilliant way of re-learning sex has, for me, been de-stigmatising non-penetrative sex. Non-penetrative sex is often understood as something preliminary, foreplay, perhaps, or just 'fooling around'. A lot of people (many under the LGBTQ+ umbrella) will discuss sex acts and dismiss them as 'not real sex' if there was no penetration. This myth is so common that it has been investigated, most recently in *"You Can Tell Just By Looking" and 20 Other Myths about LGBT Life and People*.[4] Beacon, Pellegrini and Amico discuss this myth in relation to ideas of virginity: 'culturally, we refer to a very particular sexual act – penis in vagina – as, simply, sex. Consider the expression 'losing your virginity'. This commonly means the first experience of heterosexual genital intercourse.[5] This, they argue, robs us all of important linguistic nuance. By implicitly designating non-penetrative sex as 'not sex', we lose ways of expressing our desires, legitimising our experience, and discussing our pleasure. This has ramifications outside the bedroom: the questions one is asked in a health check-up, for example, can make assumptions about what sex is, or is not. Before I developed Lichen Sclerosus, I didn't have a lot of language for sex. I certainly found talking about its nuances and boundaries tricky. Additionally, I counted as sexual partners only people I had 'proper sex' with, and counted my virginity loss as my first instance of heterosexual, penetrative sex. Part of re-negotiating my sexual identity in the wake of chronic illness has been giving space to my queer sexual experiences, re-contextualising my sex with women, and re-thinking sex with future partners of any gender.

This has been a fascinating process, and one that has certainly enlarged my vocabulary. As Bronski et al argue: 'sexual minorities – people whose sexual desires, identities, and practices differ from the norm – do a better job talking about sex, precisely because they are constantly asked to explain and justify their love and their lust to a wider culture and, even, to themselves'.[6] This has certainly been my experience. As I became slowly more confident that Lichen Sclerosus would not disbar me from a sexual future, I learnt the vocabulary to communicate this to partners. As a bisexual, I benefitted from this process enormously – I felt I was reclaiming a vocabulary that was mine by right, that I had never previously had access to. It was liberating, and a huge boost to my confidence. Learning vocabulary was fun, too, and gave me license to investigate things I had always previously felt nervous or ashamed of. I joined communities online, from FetLife to the Vulval Pain Society.[7] I listened to podcasts, from the Dan Savage Lovecast to Chase Ross and Aaron Ansuini's 'You're So Brave' podcast. I learned about different types of orgasm, and about types of intimate experience that could extend and heighten sex without even stimulating the primary sex organs, from hot wax to feathers, from massage techniques to spanking. I learned about genitals, mine and other people's, outside the gloom of the hospital. For the first time in my life I explored parts of my body that could bring me pleasure in other ways: my breasts, my neck, my ears, my ankles, my inner thighs. First by myself, then with other people. Most fun, perhaps, was buying toys I could use: I listened to the knowledgeable advice of Sh! London, the first women's sex shop in the UK.[8] About three years after diagnosis, single, and feeling as if an entirely new world had opened up, I was able to date again. It was an incredible feeling. Partners have had differing responses, but even when these have been bewildered, they've been almost entirely positive. This is, I think, partly because I'm a little more discerning now, in who I choose to be intimate with, but partly because I now have the vocabulary and knowledge to discuss sex and intimacy in ways that accurately describe my wants and needs, and acknowledge my identity as both queer and chronically ill.

It isn't, of course, plain sailing. I am not in stable remission, and haven't been for three years. My parents are still somewhat homophobic. I am often not able to bring myself pleasure, and I haven't had penetrative sex in over a year. However, I have a brilliant, kind partner, who understands the kinds of sex

I have, and who loves me for my entirety, not for the bits of me that can bring them pleasure. I am able to advocate better for the care I need in the hospital, and for the sex I want in the bedroom. I have an encyclopaedic knowledge of pleasure centres, and an impressive collection of nipple clamps. I have a good community of friends around me who are loving and supportive, and who I can talk openly with about my illness. I still, however, do not know anyone else who suffers from LS: I wonder if I ever will. Understanding sex and sexuality as a bisexual, chronically ill woman is difficult, but empowering. Allowing myself to be seen, to be 'out' in both my sexuality and my illness is scary, but it is also increasingly important. If I want to advocate for good sex and good treatment, then I want to help others to do that as well. It's an ongoing process, and I'm learning more every day. I'm hoping for remission. I'm hoping to be queer and visible and happy. I'm glad that I am as I am, because it has given me a unique opportunity to understand my body, my sexuality, myself.

by Jo Ross-Barrett

YOU HAVE THIS friend who you really like. What's tricky, though, is that things are so different between you two than they were the last time you liked someone. Even though every relationship is different, and no two sets of circumstances are alike, there are a lot of contrasts you notice with this one. It's probably at least partly because this friend of yours is a:

Girl   Non-binary person   Guy

Not that it makes a difference in how you feel. It just makes a difference in how your friend (and other people) will react to your feelings.

When you first realise how much you like your friend...

You desperately try to convince yourself that those are definitely not romantic feelings, because you don't want to be gay. This is because at your school, being gay has always been considered an even worse crime than being intelligent, and you really don't want to find out what would happen if the bullies got wind of it.

Then again, just to test the waters, you try out the labels a few times in the privacy of your head... 'Am I gay? Am I a lesbian? Maybe I'm homoromantic?' ...Nothing clicks. Even without the bias from years of homophobic schooling, it doesn't ring true when you try to claim these labels as your own.

You also don't want to get your friend in trouble with her family, who are... well, 'closed-minded' would be the most polite way to put it. You remember her anecdotes about hurtful homophobic jokes at the dinner-table, a car nearly crashing when she finally snapped and told them she was bi. Even the hypothetical notion of her being anything other than straight led to stone-cold silent treatment from people who you thought were supposed to love her unconditionally. You can't imagine her bringing you over for dinner with her parents if you ever did have that kind of relationship.

You puzzle over what you'd even call them if you ended up dating. A few Google searches later, you pick out 'datemate' as a fun option – it also nicely blends those concepts of 'just friends' and 'dating', which never really made sense as separate things from your perspective. (You're so glad you finally stumbled across the concept of relationship anarchy during your searches.)

Nbfriend is okay and you know how to pronounce it now (enby-friend), even if you're not sure of the spelling, but 'datemate' is your favourite. You hope they would like you to call them that someday.

You mull over words like 'panromantic' and 'pansexual' for a while. Are they helpful or redundant? In your case, for various reasons, they just don't quite fit right. You decide it's easier to just talk to them about your feelings directly, rather than struggling with ill-fitting labels.

♂

You briefly wonder if you're finally experiencing that moment when your hormones kick in and make you want a boyfriend. (You know, that moment some of your classmates told you to expect when you were eleven years old and about to enter high school. That moment you failed to experience for year after year after year.)

You can't help but wonder, now... Is this it? Is this what being straight feels like? But something still seems off. You flash back to your feelings for someone else once before. No less real, no less valid, and no less likely to happen again.

You roll your eyes and try to laugh off the moment of self-doubt. But you also start wearing your bi pride unicorn jewellery a lot more often, just to remind yourself that you didn't imagine it. Even though 'bisexual' or 'biromantic' isn't the right word for you, there's a certain sense of solidarity in erasure – much like the solidarity in 'invisibility' you get from wearing your ace ring.

When your friend first has an inkling about how you feel...

She assures you that you're 'not her type'. You're gutted, but you try not to show it. (Much later, you learn she tells lies like this because she doesn't want her classmates – most of whom are cis, straight, and homophobic – to be scared of her fancying them... The injustice and frustration of it all smoulders, unaddressed and unresolved, in your mind for a long time.)

♂

They don't really bring it up directly, but you notice they are more talkative than they used to be when topics such as sexuality, romance and relationships come up. You're not really sure whether this is a sign of encouragement or just a way of making sure that everyone is on the same page now that they're more comfortable with talking about this stuff. Either way, it's good to learn more about them.

♂

He invites you to a coffee shop. It should be that simple, but to other people it isn't.

Do you like him or are you just friends? Is it a date, or is it just hanging out?... Why is it that these questions are only asked by your acquaintances when it's a guy who invites you somewhere? You find yourself annoyed by the intrusiveness of their queries. Strangely, you're also frustrated by how your dates went unrecognised in the past because of their assumptions. You end up sharing a few posts about heteronormativity online, figuring that the only way such unaware people can learn about it is if the information comes directly to them.

When other people suspect you might be important to each other...

Whenever you hold hands in public, you can't help but notice the weird looks strangers give you. Some people just look curious, others look uncomfortable or downright disgusted.

You squeeze her hand a little more tightly every time. You're not entirely sure if it's to reassure yourself or her, or simply to register a small act of defiance in the face of those endless stares.

Of course, it's nothing compared to what you get at school. Even just a hug in the hallway after a rough day becomes another test of your self-restraint, as someone hurls the word 'lesbian!' at you like it's an insult. You flinch and nearly pull away, but she just holds you tighter, making sure you don't do anything reckless in response.

When your friend takes your hand on the way to a café, you're amused to see passers-by initially look right past you both. You guess you can pass for a straight couple – at least on a cursory glance – but you spot several people who do double-takes as they try to reconcile your friend's appearance with binary notions of gender.

On another occasion when you hold hands, a mutual friend of yours tries to be helpful, pointing out the well-known fact that the person you like already has a girlfriend. You don't really know what to say to that. You're pretty sure you don't actually want to replace her, or share in their romance, or even be thought of as a potential girlfriend.

You end up overcompensating a bit and enthusiastically enquiring after their girlfriend's wellbeing more than would be typical, but your friend is so head-over-heels for her that you think they don't notice anything amiss. You smile to see them so happy, noting your own total lack of jealousy. Well, whatever other people might think you feel, you're just grateful for what you've got right now.

♂

The first time you hold hands in public, you wait for the judgemental stares. Nobody looks at you twice.

The first time you kiss him in public, you're tense with paranoia that someone is going to shout abuse or throw something at you both. Nobody does.

When you mention the possibility of talking about your relationship to your mutual friends, however, it's just like you anticipated. Awkward silence, eyes reluctant to meet yours, and a level of concern for what other people think that you'd once thought only LGBTQ+ people had to worry about. (Apparently not.)

He invokes the notion of privacy. You're inclined to agree, since really your relationship is nobody's business unless they like one of you, but a creeping feeling of self-doubt nestles in your mind. You can't help but wonder if he's ashamed to be with you.

When you finally talk about it...

It takes a long time, because both of you are scared of being rejected and losing the person you admire the most. You can't imagine having to look her in the eye if it goes wrong, but you somehow summon the courage to start the most nerve-wracking conversation of your life. Thankfully, it goes well and you both laugh over the anxiety that led you to dither over your feelings for so many months.

The same evening you awkwardly confess that you like each other, you have to have a serious conversation about the prospect of hate crimes being committed against you and why it would be safer if you avoided kissing in public. It almost spoils the mood, but you're both so giddy with relief that you end up shrugging off the worry with barely a second thought.

You consider trying to formally ask them what kind of relationship they want with you. Something about that just feels unnecessary though – they seem content with the situation, and you're sure they'd let you know if anything was bothering them.

When they casually call out 'Love ya!' on their way home after a movie night, you wouldn't consider yourself surprised. You struggle with words, wondering if you can truthfully respond in kind, but they're already gone. You're relieved to realise that they don't mind precisely how you feel about them, as long as it's positive.

When you realise he likes you back, there's a burst of uncertainty about whether he'll accept the quirks of your existence. After all, your ideas about relationships involve far more practical application of queer theory and feminism than his life has ever required. You revise a list of terminology that he's unfamiliar with, preparing to explain a lot of concepts that he instinctively bundles into a one-size-fits-all model of feelings and relationships.

It's a weird conversation, but you really appreciate the fact that he pays attention to what you have to say. You tell yourself that it has to be a good sign that he genuinely wants to understand your perspective, even if he struggles to relate to a lot of your experiences. If nothing else, you're sure that it'll make for a good anecdote for one (or both) of you someday.

When it comes to telling other people...

♀

You waste no time in booking an urgent appointment with the school counsellor. Your heart beats fast and you're blushing, unsure what to expect as you blurt out the good news about the girl who likes you back. Fortunately, the counsellor doesn't make a big deal out of it, giving you a few helpful tips about coming out to your parents – apparently, drinking tea is a 'calming ritual' that can help with big surprises.

You follow the advice, making tea with shaking hands as you brace yourself to talk to your parents. Not knowing how they'll react is scary, but the blank confusion you get after your announcement is downright unsettling.

You guess you should be grateful that you're being accepted, even if not understood... After all, there are so many LGBTQ+ people who get screamed at, attacked, and even kicked out of their homes. Hell, the girl you like is so scared to tell her family – and when she eventually does, there are shouting matches and words that brand you both, burning into your minds and leaving a lifelong scar that reads FREAKS. Her once-friendly parents stare through you and never speak another word to you, even though they see you all the time.

You're lucky... at least by those standards. But you burn with envy thinking of the straight kids who are unquestioningly accepted by everyone they know. You wish everyone would treat you with that kind of respect too, but instead when you take her to parties, you are bombarded with questions. They range from the misguided to the horrifyingly personal – and seriously, if people don't know how lesbian sex works, it cannot be your responsibility to educate them. Even if a surprising number of people assume that you will. You redirect your indignant fury towards the Personal, Social and Health Education that left all of you so utterly ignorant on LGBTQ+ topics, leading to reliance on whispered gossip and embarrassing Google searches.

(Long after you break up, you read a witty retort online that you really wish you'd come up with. There was a ridiculous question you had to evade so many times: 'So who's the man in the relationship, then?' and then there was an answer on a Tumblr post: 'Neither of us – that's the whole point!' If only you had thought of that line...)

You never really need to announce your relationship status, which is probably for the best, since you don't really have a name for whatever this is. Fortunately, all of your mutual friends from uni take a very relaxed attitude to this stuff, and neither of you feels the need to mention it to family.

So although you get a few curious looks the first time you cuddle up on the sofa when your other friends are around, nobody gives you any trouble. Those who wonder, guess, or judge, are kind enough to keep their thoughts to themselves. Relief washes over you as you realise that you don't have to deal with any bigoted shouts, well-meaning condescension or innocently curious questions. It's blissful.

♂

You'd never expected to utter the words 'this is my boyfriend'. The first time you do, it's to circumvent a stupid policy where only couples should apply for a particular flat. It's a nice-looking place so you roll your eyes, make the application anyway, and practice the unfamiliar syllables until the lie almost sounds natural. It takes several more attempts before you can say it with a straight face (pun not intended).

The second occasion you ever have cause to use this phrase, it's actually true. Not that hearing the words in your own voice feels any less alien this time around... but now it's accompanied by a warm glow of tangled emotions. You note happiness, pride, confusion, the shame of betraying your own expectations, and above all, self-consciousness.

You're still not really confident that this is expressing the same truth for you that it expresses when other people say it, since your emotions straddle the supposedly-important border between platonic and romantic. But you like him, and you like your relationship, and even if the labels don't quite fit right at the moment, you're willing to give it a chance and see if you can grow into them.

When it comes to celebration...

You are given strict instructions to act like you're not an item during her birthday party, because her extended family will be there and her parents are ashamed of you both. You try not to give her parents the satisfaction of seeing how much you hate their bigotry and the power they hold over you both.

At several points you almost reach for her hand, but check yourself in the nick of time. It's a stark contrast with the time you'd held hands at your very first Pride, when you'd both felt like part of something bigger. You feel very alone in this room full of people who would love to hate you, but you cling to that memory of solidarity until you can finally make your excuses and escape.

You wander around Pride together for a while, feeling the familiar sense of solidarity in adversity along with a twinge of alienation. You share an overpriced slice of rainbow-dyed cake, the one thing you manage to twist into a symbolic form of 'representation'. As you both snack, they tell you about the difficulties of trying to connect with other trans people, only to find an obsession with binary gender again and again.

Neither of you really feels like celebrating. Having a niche identity is still difficult, even in a supportive environment like this. It's hard to feel like you belong when your identity is usually relegated to a plus sign, or shoved under the umbrella term 'queer' without your consent. Despite all that, you agree to stick around until the end of the event, hoping that eventually you'll feel at home in this community.

You invite him to Pride, trying not to take offence when he seems less than eager to attend. But then again, everyone's first Pride is a bit intimidating – the huge unknowns, the politically-charged marches, the rainbow-bedecked masses, the eternal question of 'but will I fit in if I go?' You try to chalk his reluctance up to nerves, rather than internalised homophobia... but you still have lingering doubts.

When he does make an appearance, wearing your borrowed jewellery, you're unreasonably proud of him. Perhaps that's a condescending thought, but he's come a long way since the first time you discussed orientations. Back then, his first thought was 'Why, are you interested?' and his second was 'Oh, I'm boring – I'm normal'. To his credit, after you'd explained the problems heteronormativity had caused you and your friends, he took it on board and never used the word 'normal' to describe his heterosexuality again.

When you eventually part ways...

You tell her you'd really like to stay in touch, but she calls you less and less, and eventually you stop trying altogether. The rare instances where she contacts you become momentous occasions, filled with pleasant surprise and a bitter aftertaste when you realise she's not really interested in what's going on with you.

Months after you split up, you hear the news that she has a new partner – male this time. There's a brief twinge of sadness, followed by the bittersweet realisation that this might make her life a bit easier when it comes to her family, at least for the moment. The mixture of resentment and relief is a curious feeling.

☿

You tell them you'd really like to stay in touch, but the distance makes everything a bit more difficult. You can never really think of what to say, so you trade memes and silly videos online for a while. You follow the saga of their life through Facebook posts and shared screens of the games they're playing, but it's not the same. You're glad that they seem happier, at any rate.

♂

You tell him you'd really like to stay in touch, and to your surprise he agrees. You trade messages, enthusing about shared interests and trying not to say anything that would make things awkward. You still feel a bit awkward regardless, but you reckon that's just the nature of break-ups.

When you meet up again, the sharp pang of regret catches you off-guard and you do your best to conceal how shaken you are by the sudden burst of self-doubt. The feeling takes a few days to fade away, but in the end you're content with the friendship you've managed to preserve.

Now you're moving on...

It takes a little while for you to come to terms with the way things worked out, but overall you have no regrets. Part of you wonders how things will be different the next time you like someone. You're confident that you understand yourself and what you want from life a bit better now, and hopefully that should help you find like-minded partners. At the very least, you know your approach to relationships means the number of people in the world who would be willing to try and figure out spending their lives with you is vastly smaller than the number of people who are fine with taking on more conventional relationships. On the bright side, though, you'll probably have a much better chance of things working out with people who accept or share your way of thinking. And regardless of their genders, or the kind of relationships you have, or the inherent risks of living outside the restrictions of social norms, you're confident that you'll be happier living the way that's right for you.

But there are other things that bother you.

No matter how much you grow and discover, you can't help but worry about the way wider society often seems to be stuck in a rut. The various ways people react to your partners' gender identities and presentation (as if it's a big deal that needs to be a vital aspect of how you are perceived together) isn't likely to change enough for your comfort any time soon, much as you want to help bring it to an end. Perhaps you're being too pessimistic – after all, there are plenty of people you know who constantly revise and update their ideas, especially when it comes to social norms. But for every radical new idea on the internet that brings a smile to your face, there are waves of ignorant and vicious comments that fill you with dread. You're afraid to out yourself to the general public, especially without the shield of Internet anonymity, but deep down you're sure you'll have to if you keep speaking up about the issues you care about. Even if that means dealing with harassment, threats, and even the risk of physical violence against you or someone you care about – an all too real possibility which has caused you many sleepless nights. It's a scary prospect, but you're trying to be courageous. You hope that if enough people can find hope and understanding in stories like yours, it'll be worth the risk. Maybe you can't revolutionise society overnight, but there's a chance you can help foster tolerance and understanding to ensure that at the very least, things will keep gradually improving for everyone.

however it came to be:
on being both trans and bisexual

by Naomi J Carroll

Naomi J. Carroll

As someone standing at the crossroad where bisexuality and transgender experiences intersect, I feel obligated to speak in broad strokes: to tell stories that can represent the collective communities of which I'm a part.

That, however, isn't possible.

Being just one person among a varied field of narratives, I couldn't even pretend to know how to address the variety of lives lived by my communal siblings.

I can, however, tell you about myself.

I am a woman whose heart meanders clumsily through rooms in a gallery - gazing in reverie at image after image, daring not to venture too close for fear of a fateful misstep causing harm to something priceless. Worse yet, what if upon growing attached to a masterpiece, I learn how to resent it once it's found a place in my home?

I am a gated stone archway, set in my ways and intent to weather centuries. Steady so long as no one passes through where I am most vulnerable, and could give way to collapse if prompted. I exist only a single gentle push from complete devastation.

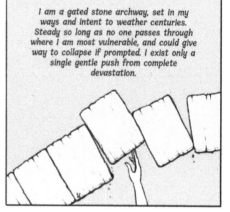

I am, however, intentional in my reclusiveness, keeping my distance from the masterpieces around me.

I am a paradox, possessing faith unshakable that there is discernible beauty in all people, yet adamant that in my own self, it is hidden beyond the capability of discovery.

Certain - whether from hubris or fear - that my worth is obscured behind quirks and idiosyncrasies, carefully laid traps that prevent even the most stubborn from surmounting them.

However it came to be, I am contented. I feel this is an important distinction to make. If only for this moment, I find no dissatisfaction in persisting as an esotery - one faint story amongst a vast and colorful field of narratives.

five times i felt invisible as a bisexual fan (and one time i didn't)

by Sarah Barnard

ONE: The Time I Had to Read Between the Lines

I AM 100% convinced that Remus Lupin is bisexual, and you cannot take this knowledge away from me. Professor Lupin, as introduced to us in *Harry Potter and the Prisoner of Azkaban*, the third instalment of the series, is gentle, brilliant, and shunned by a society who views him as unclean and dangerous because, by no fault of his own, Lupin is a werewolf. According to the author, his lycanthropy is intended as 'a metaphor for those illnesses that carry a stigma, like HIV and AIDS'. I am ready to defend J.K. Rowling on many counts, but I find it troubling that she would write a character as an AIDS metaphor, yet shoot down any suggestion from the *Harry Potter* fandom that he could be queer. There is something appropriative about it.

For the fandom uninitiated: when you love something so much you want to stay inside that world long after you have consumed and re-consumed the available content, you might start thinking about producing your own content. Yes, it's a perfectly valid form of creativity. No, it's not all about gay sex. When fans take the world and/or characters as inspiration and write stories about what happens next*, that's fanfiction. There are as many ways of being fannish as there are of being any other kind of creative, and I can guarantee there are fan-works out there on the Internet for whatever it is that you love. In this essay, I'm going to focus on fanfiction, because I'm a writer, but fandom encompasses artists, musicians, cos-players, and people making art in a hundred ways I don't even understand, for the sheer love of a story.

The practice of creating fanworks based around the romantic pairing of two characters is called ship-ping. Were I here to talk about fandom proper, rather than bisexuality through the lens of fandom, we could dig deep into the wonderful, sometimes bizarre ety-mology of fannish terms, but suffice it to say here that if you're writing stories about Sherlock Holmes and Dr John Watson Reichenbach falling for each other, you're shipping, and Holmes/Watson (or, if you prefer, Johnlock) is your ship. Personally, I am a casual multishipper, bestowing the term One True Pairing (OTP) upon my ship of the moment rather than maintaining any fierce loyalty to a beloved couple. This is not so for many others; to return to *Harry Potter*, the acrimonious wars waged between Harry/Hermione shippers and Ron/Hermione shippers are legendary. For some fans, supporting their ship is just like supporting a favourite sports team (or so

---

* or before, or during, or in an alternate universe...

I'm told – as you may have guessed, I don't really do sports). The emotions and rivalries are very serious, and intense.

I am a long-time enthusiast of the Remus/Sirius ship (two males), and also support Remus/Tonks (male and female), and believe there is no conflict between the two. My Lupin is bi, whether or not Rowling's is. (Rowling's is definitely not; like pretty much every other character, her Lupin is resolutely heterosexual, chaste until finally settling down with a partner of the appropriate sex, marrying, and producing offspring.)

In Primark with my girlfriend the other day, I asked her if I'd told her my list of characters I'd decided were bi. Being both very patient and not especially interested in clothes shopping, she told me I hadn't. 'Who's bi in *Jonathan Strange & Mr Norrell*?' I asked. It was entertaining (for me at least) but it made me realise something pretty depressing: I had to 'decide' that characters from my favourite works of fiction were bi, because otherwise, my sexuality wouldn't be represented at all.

TWO: The Time All My OTPs Were Boys Loving Boys

Not too long ago, I read a blog post asking 'Does young adult fiction hate f/f?'** YA is, like the rest of publishing, dominated by white, middle class, able-bodied narratives and writers, but its representation of LGBTQ+ teens has come on in leaps and bounds. There are even, if you look hard enough, stories

---

** *F/f being shorthand for female/female, i.e. a relationship between two female characters. Correspondingly, m/m denotes male/male pairings. M/f would be male/female, m/m/f a combination of three characters, two male and one female. I have not yet seen the shorthand used to refer to nonbinary characters, perhaps because there are still so few representations of nonbinary gender in fiction that the context of the ship would make it obvious.*

about gay black and brown teens, with one of the most celebrated titles of recent years being *Aristotle and Dante Discover the Secrets of the Universe* by Benjamin Alire Sáenz, which is about two Mexican-American teenagers. (Some readers are even inclined to claim Ari and Dante for Team Bisexual, though this is never made explicit in the text.) However, as the author of that blog post suggests, and I reluctantly agree, the rapt audience for stories about boys loving boys is just not there for bi and lesbian girls.***

Perhaps this is a question of demographics; YA is reputedly marketed mainly at teenage girls, whom statistics suggest will be majority straight. The aesthetic appeal of two boys in love is a factor missing in f/f stories. This is a theory subject to discussion and research in fan studies circles for some years, as the dynamic I am describing present in YA fiction is paralleled by the volume of fanfiction written about m/m pairings compared with f/f pairings.

We are approaching an era in YA where many of the writers being published now cut their teeth writing fanfiction, and so it is interesting to me that this privileging of male narratives is present in both environments. Male writers writing novels with queer themes based on their own lived experiences are more likely to be critically and commercially lauded than their female counterparts, but women writing queer boys are also more successful than women writing queer girls.

*** *Since my writing this, YA author Malinda Lo published her statistics on queer YA, with results that may contradict me: "My takeaway from this situation is that while publishers (major and general interest publishers) have historically published more books about cis boys, they are beginning to publish more books about cis girls." However, she notes this is a recent phenomenon and that it "remains to be seen whether the trend for cis girls continues to go up".[1]*

Internalised misogyny is almost certainly a factor. I have always been bisexual, but I have not always been a feminist, nor particularly interested in women's stories and female characters. It is, on every level, a trivial and indulgent concern, but I do worry what it says about me as a queer feminist that the fictional couples I get deeply invested in are all m/m pairs. Is some small part of me still dismissive of female characters, and instead obsessed with the pain and pleasure of the men? Or is it more the case that in pop culture, there remains a vacuum of the types of relationships between women that I find complex, compelling, worthy of burrowing down into and tapping the rich seam of 'what-if?' that fuels my favourite kind of fanfiction? Maybe I just need to reread and rewatch everything I enjoyed before my feminist awakening. I listened to *Jonathan Strange & Mr Norrell* recently, and I'm still hopelessly swooning over Jonathan Strange, but I'm also interested in Lady Pole, and the undertones of her devotion to her dear friend and fellow captive Arabella Strange.

In any case, although fandom is full of queer people, reading and writing about canonical and imagined queer relationships, some of them must be in the same place as teenage me. For some, the theory goes, exploring the sexuality of characters of another gender introduces a psychologically comforting distance. It is a safe way of engaging with non-straight sexualities, and within the constraints of heteronormative media, even in an Internet age, queering the canon might be the most accessible way of doing that.

THREE: The Time Bisexual Characters 'Didn't Like Labels'

With its openness to exploration, fandom is often a progressive space. It is not a perfect safe space by any means, but at its best it is a supportive, passionate community. Fanfiction often features trigger warnings these days. It has become a place to explore all sorts of representation issues, with headcanons**** about certain characters being trans quickly becoming adopted by large portions of the fandom. Within such small, interconnected communities, and with communication methods like Tumblr inherently structured to enable replication and reblogging, ideas catch on quickly and are shared throughout the community.

Despite this progressive streak, it is important to note that shipping is not activism. It is an unfortunate truth that some of those who enjoy consuming queer content will behave towards real life queer people in ways ranging from ambivalence to violence. It is also true that fandom offers satisfying and creative ways to subvert harmful tropes and stereotypes, to counteract the poor or non-existent representation of queer lives in fiction.

However, nominally LGBTQ+ inclusive spaces are not always welcoming to bisexuals. As bisexuality becomes more visible through the efforts of activists and creators and, yes, fans, things are getting better. But bi-erasure is still being committed by both fandom and creator. On the rare occasion that a bisexual character appears, bisexual fans seeking representation are still forced to read between the lines of characters who 'don't like labels'. As inadvisable as it is to label people with identities they have not explicitly given themselves, it is difficult to compile a list of bisexual characters without including many who are attracted to more than one gender but are never acknowledged in the text as

---

**** *Headcanon (or head canon, head-canon) is 'a fan's personal, idiosyncratic interpretation of canon, such as the backstory of a character, or the nature of relationships between characters'.*[2]

anything other than gay, or experimenting, or promiscuous, or confused. Bisexuality is still the identity that dares not speak its name.

This lack of visibility leaves me feeling conflicted about many of my favourite bisexual characters. Willow Rosenberg openly identifies herself as 'gay now!' by the final season of *Buffy the Vampire Slayer,* and as fictional as she is, it would be wrong to contradict her. She is the expert on her own sexuality. However, it was disappointing as a bisexual fan to watch this relatable character grow up, have significant relationships with men (including officially the best male character on the show, Oz), discover her own power and queerness, have significant relationships with women, and then declare herself 100% gay. This is a journey familiar to many gay women, and it is of course completely valid. I am happy to surrender Willow to the lesbian camp, but it stings a little.

Alana Bloom, from NBC's *Hannibal,* is initially part of a love triangle between troubled FBI investigator Will Graham, and the eponymous Dr Lecter. (It being *Hannibal,* it's a lot more complicated than that, but that's not the point.) After turning Will down, she embarks on an ill-advised affair with Hannibal. And then, in season three, she meets Margot Verger, marries her, has a son with her, and gets the hell out of Dodge. There's a weird kaleidoscope sex scene in the mix there too. Alana is absolutely, unquestionably bisexual. It has been confirmed by the writers and stars. But it's never remarked upon in-universe. In some ways, this is progress – it's not remarked upon because this is a show about a cannibal and Alana, although a series regular, is a peripheral character. One would assume the circles she runs in are pretty liberal, and mostly do not care about her sexuality, having more pressing concerns like not getting eaten on their minds. Most of the characters have known each other for years; a line revealing her bisexuality would be forced. But the trope of bisexuals never being named as such persists.

FOUR: The Time Shipping Made Straight Characters Gay

One of the main problems faced by fanfiction writers pairing off, for example, the two male leads of a show, is what to do with the canonical female love interest. There is an ignoble tradition prevalent in such fanfiction of erasing women from narratives, although as feminist critiques become more widespread, fandom is markedly more disdainful of this practice than I remember it being in my teenage years. Characters are rarely explicitly identified as straight in canon, but heteronormativity means fans are left to assume so. Where this assumption is left unquestioned, it results in tropes such as 'gay for you', where the (male) main character is indeed straight, but makes an exception for the (male) love interest.

There are some male main characters subject to fairly widespread headcanon that they are bisexual, from Steve Rogers, more commonly known as Captain America, and Dean Winchester from The CW's long-running fantasy series *Supernatural*, to the narrator of Donna Tartt's *The Secret History* (trust me on this, there is *no way* he's not into Francis). Where the female characters are left intact, and their relationships with the men being shipped are given the appropriate respect, the fanwork is able to explore sexuality with greater complexity. Sometimes that might mean exploring compulsory heterosexuality and societal pressures, and sometimes we end up with nuanced, honest representations of bisexuality. Of course, it might be that writers are cautious about representing bisexual characters as cheaters, because that perpetuates stereotypes of the greedy, unfaithful bisexual.

FIVE: The Time Shipping Made Gay Characters Straight

When the opposite happens, in other words, when characters portrayed in same-sex relationships are portrayed in fandom in opposite-sex relationships, fandom is much more resistant. A lot of this resistance is from a desire to respect lesbian characters' identity, and avoid the harmful trope of the 'right man' being able to 'cure' women of this aberrant identity. LGBTQ+ representation is still so rare that it is genuinely harmful to attempt to erase the identities of the queer characters that do exist. I am sympathetic to the view that lesbian characters and the queer fans who identify with them ought to be protected from this kind of violence.

However, some of this reluctance is, in my opinion, the result of biphobia. Bisexual people in relationships that 'pass as straight' are a less-than kind of queer. By this logic, a woman who has previously expressed interest only in women is a lesbian, whether she has declared this identity or not; if you write her falling in love with a man, you are taking away her queerness. You are taking away her history. You are taking away her identity.

This attitude is born of a desire to negate the queerness of bisexuality. It is harmful, reductive, and unfortunately prevalent. Women who love women face enormous harm at the hands of a violent heteronormative patriarchy, but surely there is a way to respect that truth without erasing the identities of the millions of queer women who sometimes love men.

I AM A BISEXUAL FAN

Like many of my bisexual peers, I adopted all sorts of different identity labels not only while I was growing up, but well into my late teens and twenties. I didn't really have private access to the internet until I was eighteen, which in some ways was a blessing; I wouldn't wish unfettered social network access on teen me, even the limited versions that existed a decade ago. However, it did mean that it wasn't until after my coming of age (theoretically, at least) that I began to encounter the smorgasbord of identities that today's teens are familiar with. For about four years, a period of time coinciding directly with my time at university, I used Tumblr pretty much daily. It was a crash course in all things gender and sexuality, and among the pile-ons, misinformation, memes and drama, I learnt a lot. What was homoromantic demisexual, and was I one? In a phrase familiar to anyone seeking bisexual representation from fictional characters, I decided for a long time that I didn't like or need labels, comfortable to call myself 'not straight' (the one thing I was actually certain about by this point) or maybe 'queer'.

I have always been bi, if not always sure about calling myself that. I have also always been fannish. Preteen Sarah wrote herself into *Animorphs* and *Pokemon* fanfiction, obsessively copied down *Digimon* stats and *Yu-Gi-Oh!* ship names. Over the years, I have been part of fandoms you couldn't avoid knowing exist (*Harry Potter, Game of Thrones*) and fandoms a little further off the beaten path (UK politics during the 2010 general election). It would be overly simplistic and, I think, false to say I 'discovered myself' through fandom, or even to suggest that I found a community there that I didn't have in the real world. But fandom did – *does* – help me explore facets of myself and develop skills and understanding that are transferrable to my endeavours outside fandom.

I would be a less confident writer without the in-depth discussions I have had about character motivations or the enthusiastic responses to my (extremely sporadic) fanworks. Fandom taught me to critically engage with the media I consume, and that to do so is rewarding, even important. It also gave me access to a vast range of representations of LGBTQ+ lives and love that simply weren't present in the mainstream media I was consuming at the time. Even in 2017, where queer media proliferates as the sources splinter into independent outlets, and readers and viewers – fans – have more power to actively participate in the creation of the media they are interested in consuming (an example is the book you are currently holding in your hands). Even now, there are few places you will find the kind of passionate, heart-breaking, domestic, normalised queer themed fiction that fandom specialises in.

As fandom continues to enter into exploratory dialogue with text and creator, and as fans become creators of their own canon, we will continue to see sensitive and thoughtful representations of all identities. Shipping is not activism, but writing stories in which my favourite characters fall in love with others of all genders is an affirmation. *We exist*. Transformative works can twist the canon into something a little more like the world I know. More bisexual fanfiction for all!

a place to 'b'

by Laura Clay

IT'S QUITE HARD to write about being bisexual when I don't exist.

In fact, for nearly twenty years I haven't existed. I've been drifting around watching conversations happen as if I'm not there, wondering if I'm allowed to join in, like a queer Scrooge led around by the Ghost of Sexualities Past. But my bisexuality has always been an incontrovertible fact. I've known since the first time I put Angelina Jolie on my desktop wallpaper when I was fourteen. It's something I'm frank and open about these days, but it's taken a long time to fight my way there, and we're still nowhere near able to throw off our cloaks of invisibility.

To mark 2017's Pride season, and celebrate the fiftieth anniversary of the partial decriminalisation of homosexuality, a range of special TV and radio shows was commissioned. While many I watched were fantastic bits of social history, bisexuals barely got a mention. I waited on every documentary to mention our existence, but most shows seemed to focus on the L and G in LGBTQ+, to the exclusion of everything else. In fact, the only wholly bi documentary in the entire BBC Gay Britannia season was a single show tucked away on the World Service. One show. It sometimes feels like bisexuals were the kids picked last for the school sports teams, in favour of the trendier gays and lesbians.

This lack of decent representation has had a great impact on my personal life, as I've struggled over choosing to be visible in the first place. I had my first sexual experience with a girl at university, but decided not to make her my first girlfriend, because I was worried about what people would think. Cambridge was an odd beast like that. If you were a rich white gay man, go for it! After all, there were many students that had laid that path for you, and I was at a few formal dinners where fellows would openly boast about their encounters. If you were a bisexual woman? Well, we had one paragraph in the student union women's handbook. Would that do?

Workplaces, too, have been a mixed bag for being visibly bi. Co-workers at more technical jobs just shrugged and carried on as normal. But one office, the living embodiment of the sort of people who think 'Oh mate, you're Archbishop of Banterbury' is a way of life, responded with the most horrific biphobia I've ever heard. After that, being invisible felt like the safer option.

It's no surprise, then, that I didn't go to my first Pride until 2016. I was only convinced in the end because my husband and a bi friend came with me. It should have felt liberating, thrilling even, to walk in a sea of rainbows among others who shared my identity. But I was terrified. Terrified of being spotted by close friends and family, to whom I wasn't out. Terrified of other people's judgement. Terrified about the stories I'd heard of prejudice toward bisexuals within Pride itself. I cried my eyes out in that crowd. I felt part of something and utterly alone at the same time.

It's a simple problem: if your existence isn't shown regularly and presented as normal with no fanfare, nobody will know you're there at all. Sure, we've had Anna Friel's much-lauded lesbian kiss on *Brookside*; we've had *Queer as Folk*, and a gay *Doctor Who* companion, but writers seem to routinely forget about bisexual characters. This has been admitted by BBC drama boss Oliver Kent in a recent *Huffington Post* article, where he states 'I don't think we've quite got [bisexual representation] right yet as often as we could. You don't want the sexuality to be the story, and yet if you hide it too much, it's not part of the story at all.'[1] In the rare event that we *do* feature in the media we consume, no matter how harmfully we're portrayed, it's lauded as 'progress'. Job done, diversity box ticked, stop complaining.

I write for young adults, and in general I've found that teenage fiction is some of the most LGBTQ+-friendly, boundary-pushing literature out there. That said, bisexuality is still overshadowed by gay/lesbian characters and plots, and when we do appear, it's not always well-received by the very vocal YA readership. One fantasy author recently proclaimed that she was very diverse because she had a bi character in her latest book. It turned out that this character only existed to invite a man and a woman to a threesome – hardly a shining example of representation. This is an issue I try hard to make right in my own writing; my current main character is a bisexual girl, because I want to write the realistic, honest books I wish my teenage self could have read.

To battle invisibility and misinformation, we must shout louder than the voices trying to drown us out. A difficult task, when the well-worn tropes that bisexuals are 'sitting on the fence', are 'going through a phase', or are somehow 'greedy', informs those who should be helping us. Of course, the media remain the prime culprits as usual. Consider Amber Heard's treatment in the tabloids. A story that should've been as simple as 'Johnny Depp abused his wife' swiftly became 'it was her fault because she was bi' and 'well, she was warned that coming out would end her career'. Bisexuality, it seems, is still something wheeled out to shock, displayed as a defect, and so feeds our shame and guilt.

Recently, I joined the Order of Perpetual Indulgence as one of their 'henches', after a close friend persuaded me. The Order, founded in San Francisco in 1979, works to raise awareness of sexual intolerance, promote safe sex, and raise money for LGBTQ+ organisations. I'd agreed to help them out at Fife's first ever Pride, and had no idea what to expect. It was only my third time at a march; I was just beginning to feel like it was acceptable for me to be there in the first place.

If you'd told me I'd start the day sitting on a sofa nervously drinking cheap wine from the bottle and having glitter blown onto my face, and end it standing on stage after the parade with my fellow Order members, paying tribute to those lives lost to AIDS and hate crimes, I'd have laughed. But I somehow found the courage to make it happen, and it went down so well we couldn't walk two steps without being stopped and asked for pictures. It felt like being on the most awesome family day out in the world – because the Order *is* a family, and a supremely tolerant and loving one at that. I was literally centre-stage with fellow bisexuals. You couldn't get more visible than that.

Because of my new position, I was asked about my experiences as a bi woman at our events. I helped out at an 'elevation', where postulants and novices move up in the Order as a result of good deeds in the LGBTQ+ community. One of the spectators in the pub was a student who ended up chatting to us and asking about what the Order does. The moment I realised my role as a bisexual henchperson was important was when he peered at a badge on my uniform and said 'So, you're bi? That's cool. Lots of my girlfriends have been bi. I guess everyone's open about it now.' Everyone, I replied, except those who can't for fear of receiving abuse, losing their jobs, being shunned by loved ones, or experiencing violence. He looked genuinely appalled by this, and ended up staying to talk for over an hour about biphobia, bi visibility, and safe sex. Thanks to this, he left more informed and promising to bring his queer aunt to our next event. Job (partly) done.

This year, I've been to two Prides and am gearing up for a third in Glasgow. I believe that my presence as a bisexual at these events is more necessary than ever. In the coming months, I'm planning on involving myself in more LGBTQ+ campaigning, with a view to eventually becoming a fully fledged 'sister' in the Order. After all, it's hard to ignore a person in a full nun's habit wearing makeup straight from an 80s New Romantic's handbag. It's much easier to talk about being bisexual when your existence is validated in such a public way. The process to personal visibility has taken me twenty years, but I feel like I've now found a platform where I can make my voice heard. I just hope it doesn't take another twenty years to get the job done for everyone else hiding in the shadows of bi prejudice.

girlfriend wanted:
bisexuals need not apply

by Viola Orson

LET'S START THIS essay with a disclaimer: I am not bisexual. But like a fair number of lesbians, I started my coming out story identifying as one. If you were to walk into a gay bar tonight and informally poll the lesbian population there, my bet is that quite a few women would raise their hands and admit to a similar trajectory: bi to gay. While this isn't a scientific measure by any stretch of the imagination, from my conversations with other lesbians and my consumption of a ridiculous amount of lesbian books, movies, and television, I would say it's a common experience.

Now, in my opinion, this isn't necessarily a problem. I owe a debt of gratitude to the bisexual community for having tried on their label. Eventually, I found that I was mostly using it as an excuse to date women, had several moments of wide-eyed realisation – many while consuming the aforesaid lesbian media – and then officially came out as a lesbian. As someone raised in a fairly traditional household, initially identifying as bisexual helped me in my first baby steps toward becoming more myself.

My experiences trying on the label taught me a lot. Namely: holy shit, are some lesbians awful toward bisexual women. As someone with no gaydar or really any social skills to speak of, I started my first forays into dating via online sites. There was a common phrase that I saw many lesbians put on their dating profiles, often to the effect of 'If you're bisexual, you can fuck right off'. Some profiles were more tactful about it, but they were still essentially requesting that a whole group of potential dates should go shove it where the sun doesn't shine, and it was an odd preference I couldn't understand. In my early days, identifying as bisexual, I immediately clicked off those profiles and decided to keep my strongly worded rebuttals to myself. I continued to do this after relabelling myself as well, as I didn't get why someone would be so vehemently opposed to dating a bisexual. The more I paid attention, the more I heard this sentiment reflected elsewhere as I explored 'the community'. It recurred consistently in various formats, as either a serious issue or one that could be seen as a joke and satirised. Seeing such a common theme in online dating profiles, lesbian movies, YouTube videos, and in casual conversations got me thinking. I've come up with a theory about why it's so prevalent.

My theory stems from a common factor that I've noticed amongst lesbians: we *really* like being lesbians. And I'm not just talking about the lady-lovin' part of that, which is pretty great. Being a lesbian comes along with a lot of ideas about what being a lesbian means: wearing plaid, the compulsory adoption of cats on at least an annual basis, certain political views, certain ways of talking or walking (looking at you, butch lesbians). We're pretty caught up in all the trappings surrounding that label, when at its core, 'lesbian' means one thing: 'a homosexual woman' (according to the Oxford Dictionary). But we love the stereotypes, to an almost ridiculous degree. It's a simple fact in itself, but the *idea* of being a lesbian and the accompanying connotations are the source of the problem that lesbians seem to have with bisexual women. There are approximately three schools of thought among the lesbian community, as it were: that bisexuals are either straight women who want attention (the 'sexual tourist'), lesbians who are too repressed to admit they're lesbians (the 'repressed lesbian'), or just fence-sitters who want to enjoy both worlds but commit fully to neither (the 'chimera'). These three stereotypes are fairly enmeshed in each other, so allow me to deconstruct them a bit.

The first school of thought arises from a common problem in the lesbian community: the straight girl who is more than happy to lead an equally willing lesbian along, all the while claiming that she thinks she might be bisexual. Once the situation falls apart, the straight girl goes back to being straight and the lesbian goes back to being grumpy (possibly now with another cat or two). The lesbian now associates this girl with *all* bisexuals and assumes that *any* girl that says she is bisexual will do this do her. This stereotype may come from direct experience, or be passed down as a cautionary campfire story that the butch lesbians tell the baby lesbians. I know this because that's how I first heard it. While there wasn't actually a campfire around, I definitely had some friendly warnings from my elders to watch out for the sexual tourist. I not only heard this from people that I knew, but I've seen it in movies, short films, and YouTube videos. It can often be presented as a joke (see 'The Six Lesbians You'll Date Before You Die'), but also as a serious problem.

The second school of thought applies to me in a way that hits a little too close to home: the bisexual that is too repressed to admit she's a lesbian. *C'est moi.* I did – eventually – admit that I was gay and happily exchange one label for another that fit more accurately. There are quite a number of lesbians who do this, as I have said before. Some of them, however, maintain the mentality that bisexuality is just a step to either becoming a 'fully-fledged' lesbian or running and hiding back in the closet. This stereotype is a symptom, however, of a deeper problem: xenophobia. This fear of outsiders has historical precedence, warranted or not, and the bisexual community is the most recent focus of this fear. The big connecting factor between these three schools of thought is the sense that bisexual women are somehow cheating the system. Xenophobic fear and the desire for exclusivity fuel the stereotypes, which in turn become an excuse for prejudiced behaviour.

Rather than viewing 'bisexual' as a label unto itself, there's also a strong belief that bisexuals are a chimera: half straight and half gay. I've heard a number of lesbians joke with their bisexual friends that they are 'half gay,' and that this lets them in on some 'lesbian secrets'. Those situations are typically light-hearted, but this idea of being half gay is a double-edged sword. When it's used to include people and open a community to them, I have fewer problems with it. However, the other side of this idea is used to shut bisexual women out: they are only '*half* gay' and as a result, enjoy the privileges of being 'half straight'. There's an insidious idea that they get to 'turn off' being gay and can choose to be straight, thus making bisexuals interlopers into a secret gay world. This very idea is what first convinced me to come out as bisexual; my thinking was that I could acknowledge the 'gay half' of myself and still have a 'straight half'. After considerable time spent thinking and discussing, I did realise that I was a lesbian. My experience is not a unique one, either. Because this is such a common story, the mentality is: 'Why won't they just come out and admit that they're gay?' Sometimes this is expressed in jest, but there are so many lesbians who have used bisexuality as the gateway drug to lesbianism that it has led to general mistrust of bisexual women. This viewpoint is entrenched in the lesbian community.

The 'chimera' bisexual, and really all three stereotypes I've outlined, tie together with this general mistrust of bisexual women. The feeling that bisexuals are outsiders in the community is often summed up in the belief that 'bisexual women are sluts'. It's been a culturally common assumption for as long as the idea of bisexuality has been expressed, and lesbians are just as prone to believe it as the Bible-thumping, hellfire-and-brimstone-preaching old lady down the street. This belief is tricky though, because it's a bit of a Schrödinger's Cat: the bisexual both exists and doesn't exist at the same time. The woman is bisexual, because she is at least flirting with another woman, but she's simultaneously not, because her hetero side negates her queerness. This is where the 'sexual tourist' stereotype and the chimera stereotype come into play: whether she's straight or just 'half straight,' she is still straight somehow. There's a certain amount of resentment among some lesbians because they feel that bisexuals are floating between worlds, enjoying the privileges of both while avoiding the problems that many lesbians have to deal with – namely, having to be gay and face the discrimination of being 'fully other' all the time. The bisexual, they feel, can 'turn on' being gay and enjoy flings with women while still enjoying heteronormative privilege. It's the reason why, when I came out to my parents, they hoped that I could at least be bisexual, rather than 'fully gay'. These ideas all coexist in some strange kind of double-think: the bisexual woman is leading on the lesbian, who has been honest about her feelings towards women, while the bisexual is lying to herself since she is repressed, or attention-seeking, or commitment-phobic, or all of the above.

Something I noticed in trying to join my university's LGBTQ+ club was that lesbians (at least the ones enthusiastic enough to join the club) were very concerned about being lesbians. There was always some discussion about how they would be treated by other people who weren't LGBTQ+. I would be the last person to say that isn't an issue – I'm even writing under a pseudonym, and my whole situation... that's complicated. But here's the problem as I observed it: in being so concerned with how others were treating them, they weren't paying attention to how they were treating others. In being wrapped up with 'lesbian issues' of societal acceptance, discrimination, and most importantly, lesbian identity, they often overlooked bisexual issues, or even trivialised them. This idea that bisexuals can exist in two worlds so easily and enjoy the privileges of appearing heterosexual has led to the assumption that bisexuals are somehow excluded from the sort of discrimination that lesbians have to face.

The three stereotypical ideas I've mentioned are all entwined with each other. I was reading a 'Dear Prudence' advice column recently about a lesbian who was upset that her wife insisted on identifying as bisexual.[1] People wanted to ask her opinion on an issue 'as a lesbian' and she would respond that she was actually bisexual. This letter perfectly encapsulates the problem that lesbians have with bisexual women: the feeling that they just want attention from men, that they're leading on the lesbian, that they don't have the same connection to the discrimination that lesbians face, that they're lying to themselves about actually being gay – it's all there in one messy agony aunt letter. The attitude of the writer is more confused than anything else; there is a sense of 'She married me, therefore, she is a lesbian now'. A quick Google search led me to a tsunami of articles or similar letters – some of them from bisexual women – about this feeling that the gender of the person they choose as a life partner in turn determines their sexual orientation, once and for all. *That's it, she married a man, and so she's straight now. She will never ogle another pair of amazing boobs ever again.* First of all, everyone looks at boobs, so that's outrageous. Secondly, that's not how attraction works. In a lot of ways, if any of these stereotypes are given a second of thought, they each fall apart. The inherent contradictions and twists have sort of buttressed the fear of bisexuals as a whole, like a horrifying prejudice castle. Can someone really be 'half straight' and 'half gay,' or is the reality of sexual expression more complicated than that?

Many of the main ideas behind negative bisexual stereotypes are more indicative of lesbian fears and insecurities than rooted in any fact. Ultimately, the lesbian community has taken the fear of prejudice from straight 'outsiders', and applied it to the bisexual community based on this idea that they are 'half straight', lying about being straight, or using the privilege of appearing heteronormative. This attitude completely overlooks the problems a bisexual person faces – and for a community that claims to be welcoming,

inclusive, and open-minded, perpetuating these stereotypes becomes hypocritical.

I've watched the nonsensical ostracism of bisexuals from a
fairly comfortable distance. After a brief and somewhat recurring attempt to join the LGBTQ+ club at university, I couldn't
help but feel a certain ridiculousness in some of the attitudes
prevailing there. There was a genuine sense of community
and a desire to protect each other, which was the main reason
I tried to attend regularly. With any group, though, there is
always a danger of developing an 'us versus them' mentality.
With such diverse subsections of people included within
'LGBTQ+,' there is a tendency towards factionalism. While
this has certainly improved in recent years (see the pre-1990s
relationship between gay men and lesbians), it still contrib-
utes to ongoing bisexual stereotyping and discrimination. I
met many people who defined everything they thought, said,
and did by the label they had chosen for themselves, rather
than allowing their sexual identity to be an integrated part
of who they are. Think of all the labels lesbians have for the
different 'types' based on personal style: butch, diesel dyke,
fem, lipstick, baby butch, and probably a million others. One
dating website I signed up for, which was specifically for lesbian and bisexual women, had you choose which type you
were. Friends and people I know have asked me this question too. On the flip side, how many straight people have you
asked 'Which type are you?' like they're a Pokémon?

Granted, things like clothing and personal style have often
been important cultural shorthand, identifying the members
of a group. I would ask that people think on this, though: how
often has this led to a factionalist attitude? Groups require
conformity, regardless of what their beliefs are, because of
their very nature: a group has a central, unifying goal. I would

say the goal of the LGBTQ+ community is positive, but the reason for this group's very existence comes with its own set of problems. What makes the LGBTQ+ group identification necessary in the first place is the pervasive, wider cultural mentality that there is 'normal' sexuality and gender identity and there is 'other'. And think of all the people that are included in 'other': homosexuals, bisexuals, transgender, asexual, queer, questioning, intersex, and allies. That adds up to quite a group of people, all with varied histories, nuanced beliefs about themselves and the world around them, interesting stories and perspectives – but I feel that all that humanity is swept away by slapping a label on someone and saying 'This is you now!' The LGBTQ+ community has come a long way since people began defining 'normal' and 'other', and there are still many steps that need to be taken to ensure that members of this community can even have personal safety. There is still a worthy purpose in activism. But this doesn't mean that the community as a whole shouldn't take a good, long look at itself and fix its own problems with stereotyping.

I have seen more than just the negative side of the community, to be fair. But those who want some kind of exclusive lesbian club – no boys or bisexuals allowed – seem, at least to me, to be the loudest voices. They are at least the most visible because, relying again on stereotypes, many of those people fit the expectations of what it means to be a lesbian. And the biggest stereotype of all is really, *really* caring that everyone knows you're a lesbian. Ultimately, though, a label is a place to start, and that can lead to a more realistic understanding of yourself. It did for me. I fit very neatly into my own theory about the lesbian mentality towards bisexuals: I was the 'repressed lesbian'. I began with one label and had to evaluate for myself whether it fit and to what extent. I then chose another which fit me more closely. A label is just the easiest and simplest way to sum up a part of who a person is: the person underneath is always more nuanced than the label they've adopted.

Through my observations trying to understand bisexual discrimination from the lesbian community, I've come to believe that those who buy into the minutiae surrounding what it means to be a lesbian have been swept along by its prejudices as well. Hence, the 'no bisexuals need apply' mentality that some lesbians have towards bisexual women. My theory, though, is just that: a theory. I've pulled some of the threads to try to untangle the ways that bisexual discrimination is justified, but the mind-sets that I have tried to explain are the shadows on the wall. The concept of what it means to be a lesbian deeply relates to feeling outside of the benefits of real or perceived heteronormativity and being part of another group entirely. The bisexual as a sort of straight sexual tourist, repressed lesbian, or 'half gay, half straight' interloper all tie into the fear that bisexuals are somehow gaming the system by having ties to the heterosexual world and its privileges. In defining 'What does it mean to be a lesbian?' many have unyielding ideas about who should have access to – or simply be included in – that community in the sense of a shared goal or struggle. The lesbian community struggles to fairly include bisexual women based on the aspects of bisexual identity that are uncomfortable for them to accept. But our identities themselves are more individual than any singular label we apply to ourselves or others. The lesbian community in particular needs to re-evaluate how labels have become a way to define and divide people, rather than a simple way to introduce a multifaceted and deeply personal identity. The more critical we are of these labels, the more we can be aware of the differences between the conveniently straightforward ways we present ourselves and the complex human beings we are underneath.

on being black and bi-furious

by Jayna Tavarez

I HADN'T GIVEN much thought to dating or relationships or love, until I started dating my first boyfriend my freshman year of high school. I was straight, I guess. I mean… Sure, if I thought someone was cute, then they were cute, but it's not like anyone caught my eye enough to cause me to push back against my heteronormative socialisation. That was true, at least, until I finally challenged myself to leave my then-boyfriend, and with that, opened my sexuality up to be challenged by others.

'Jay… You're either straight or you're a lesbian. You gotta pick a side eventually.'

'I mean –'

'Are you straight?'

'No, you know I'm not, but –'

'So you're a lesbian?'

'No, but I –'

'You know you can't play both sides forever, right?'

This was one of many conversations I had with a close friend of mine, who identifies as a Black, masculine-presenting, lesbian woman. It was my senior year of college, and I had just ended a long-term relationship with another Black, masculine-presenting, lesbian woman. We made each other pretty happy, with the exception of one question that would always start a massive argument that ultimately led to our breakup:

'If you're as committed to spending the rest of your life with me as you say you are, why is it so hard to tell people you're a lesbian?'

Apparently, 'because I'm not a lesbian' wasn't sufficient. Upset, I went to my close friend, who I hoped would provide me with some post-breakup comfort. Yikes. Bad idea.

'I just don't understand. It's like she doesn't trust me...'

'Can you really blame her though? I mean, you could never understand the shit that straight girls put us through...'

'What? How can I be straight? I'm bisexual, at the least, even though I don't like that term.'

'There's no such thing as bisexual – well, there is, but it's usually just a phase for girls who either aren't ready to come out yet or are just waiting for the right dude. Either way, you need to figure it out sooner than later. You can't just lead people on. This is why I hate dating girls who aren't lesbians.'

I had never been so angry. Out of all of my conversations with her, this was it. This was the one that did it. This was the conversation that drove me to interrogate my sexuality, and more importantly, my relationship with bisexuality. After I removed myself from that conversation, I grappled with so many thoughts that for years, I had refused to unpack. I craved a sense of community within LGBTQ+ spaces, but

I was still very uncomfortable identifying as bisexual, and a little part of me knew that it was probably for the best that I didn't. I couldn't put my finger on why that was. When I was asked about my sexuality, I let people make assumptions about it based on who I was dating at the time, and I was very selective about who and how I corrected. I needed to ask myself: why am I so opposed to being bisexual? Am I opposed to *being* bisexual – or am I opposed to 'bisexual' as a label? Maybe I don't like labels? Maybe it's *that* label, but why?

I buried myself in the literature: blogs, opinion pieces, Twitter rants, anything I could find. There were so many conversations happening. What is bisexuality? Is it the same as pansexuality? Is bisexuality transphobic? Is 'bisexual privilege' a thing? I was learning so much about other bisexual people's experiences, and it was incredibly validating, knowing that I wasn't alone in my frustration. I had just entered my first semester of graduate school, and decided that I wanted to commit the next two years to doing my thesis research on bisexuality. Next stop: JSTOR.

From the research that I gathered, I found that bisexual people experience a unique type of marginalisation within the LGBTQ+ community. Bisexual women in particular were reported to experience elevated levels of stress, isolation and exclusion, and mental health concerns.[1] Bisexual activists and researchers coined the term biphobia, a word I had never heard before, for the prejudice against people who identify as bisexual or do not identify within the gay/straight binary.[2] Bisexuality as a sexual orientation is unique because it challenges mainstream heteronormative ideas, while also creating a rift in LGBTQ+ communities by challenging standards of a 'right' or 'ideal' type of LGBTQ+ identity.[3] While heterosexism impacts all LGBTQ+-identified people, biphobia is rooted in both heteronormativity and monosexism, which impacts bisexual people specifically.[4] Once I understood the difference between homophobia and biphobia, it suddenly made sense why bisexual people held such a complicated position within the community.

I stumbled on a very interesting case study that helped me understand the complicated relationship between bisexual and lesbian women specifically. Between 1989 and 1993, the Northampton Pride March Steering Committee debated whether 'bisexual' should be included in the march title. While there was already existing tension between bisexual and lesbian women, this tension was exacerbated when, for the first year ever, 'bisexual' was included in the march's title, and there were no lesbian speakers at the march. Those who were pro-inclusion felt that 'bisexual' deserved to be included in the name of the march. They saw the name change as an opportunity for coalition building across a wide range of sexual identities. Meanwhile, those who were pro-exclusion believed that the march had a traditionally lesbian focus and should be dedicated specifically to lesbian feminist politics. Pro-exclusion lesbians argued that bisexual women should build and develop their own bisexual communities and politics, and pro-inclusion bisexual women argued that they were asking for formal inclusion in a history they had always been a part of.[5]

In 1991, the Gay and Lesbian Community Action Council conducted the first Bisexual Community Needs Assessment to compile a report listing the wants and needs of bisexual people involved in lesbian and gay activism in the Twin Cities of Minnesota. After interviewing 38 bisexual men and women, the assessment found that participants generally expected more acceptance from the gay and lesbian community than the heterosexual community, which made exclusion from lesbian and gay spaces more hurtful and isolating. Several of the bisexual women noted that they were condemned or excluded, asked to leave lesbian groups, and were discouraged or outright prohibited from speaking at women's conferences.[6]

And over twenty years later, the 2012 Bisexual Community Needs Assessment could easily be misidentified as the one from 1991. It found that bisexual people still felt a lack of solidarity and inclusion within lesbian and gay communities. One bisexual woman working at an LGBTQ+ organisation reported being consistently read as straight and was asked how she got a job for the organisation as an ally. Another reported that she was consistently referred to as Lesbian Lite™. There was also a significant gap between how closely bisexual people *wanted* to feel connected to the LGBTQ+ community, and how closely they *actually* felt connected to the LGBTQ+ community, solidifying the disconnect between bisexual needs and bisexual realities.[7]

After reading everything I could find, I was excited to finally conduct my own interviews. I reached out to bisexual Twitter and Facebook pages asking them to share and retweet my study. I was flooded with over 150 responses from bisexual and pansexual women, woman-aligned, and non-binary people who were interested in participating in my study. I felt so validated!... and then, suddenly, really discouraged. Out of 186 interested participants, only 46 identified as people of colour – and only 9 identified as Black. I went back to both of the assessments: 1991, 89% white. 2012, 91% white. Yikes, okay. How ironic was it that my experiences as a Black bisexual woman navigating these intersections drove me to conduct this entire study, just to feel isolated in my own work? Why do LGBTQ+ organisations struggle to find and include bisexual people of colour? Why is there no research on the ways that the intersection of race impacts the way bisexual people experience biphobia? We need to talk about the racialisation of biphobia.

LGBTQ+ organisations and activist groups being inclusive of bisexual people is critical for the success of the movement. Lesbian women, gay men, and bisexual people reportedly make up only 3.5% of the United States population, and of that 3.5%, bisexual people lead at 52%.[8] Additionally, it is estimated that over one million African-American adults in the United States identify as LGBTQ+.[9] Black bisexual people exist, and our intersections make a difference.

One day, I'll do a Bisexual Community Needs Assessment that focuses specifically on bisexual people of colour, because I believe that understanding the intersections of our identities is critical in creating a more welcoming, supportive, and inclusive community for us. Until then, here are some of my recommendations:

1. Intersectional bisexual-specific research. The lack of research I found reinforced that the erasure I felt was indicative of a larger problem. Although there is limited data specifically on bisexual people, there are several studies that focus specifically on bisexual mental health. However, we also need research analysing the sociological conditions that allow for the marginalisation of bisexual people to even exist. Additionally, there is limited research on the experiences of being Black and bisexual outside of an HIV/AIDS context. Having data specifically on bisexual people of colour is necessary so that our experiences can be accurately represented, too.

2. Intentional outreach to bisexual people of colour. As hype as I was every time I found a journal article or book about bisexuality, I was disappointed at how overwhelmingly white the participants were. It was hard to feel holistically connected to those experiences when there was no conversation around the racialisation of biphobia and its impact on mental health, sense of community, and sense of identity. It's not enough to acknowledge that they wish they had bisexual people of colour in their study – bisexual organisations and researchers doing work around bisexuality need to be intentional about including bisexual people of colour, and refuse to accept anything less.

3. Increased funding for both bisexual organisations and organisations that serve LGBTQ+ communities of colour. Bisexual organisations receive a significantly lower amount of funding compared to other LGBTQ+ organisations. According to the Funders for LGBTQ Issues' 2015 tracking report, LGBTQ+ communities of colour receive roughly 14 percent of total LGBTQ+ funding, and the bisexual community receives less than one percent.[10] Continuing to provide limited funding for LGBTQ+ organisations that serve LGBTQ+ communities of colour, and practically no funding for bisexual-specific organisations reinforces the limited support for bisexual people, and specifically bisexual people of colour. That's not okay, especially considering that bisexual people of colour are more likely to experience stressors, such as poverty and mental health issues.

4. Intersectional bisexual-specific resources, programming, and education. Bisexual people are consistently forced to rely on the gay and lesbian community for access to resources. In the 1991 assessment, participants noted that they had to validate their own identities with minimal outside support.

As previously noted, biphobia is different from homophobia, and the experiences of bisexual people of colour are different from those of white bisexual people due to additional racial marginalisation. Bisexual-specific resources, programming, and education is necessary in affirming bisexual identities and encouraging bisexual people of colour to be involved in white lesbian- and gay-dominated spaces.

5. Increased visibility for bisexual people of colour. Bisexual people have always struggled with visibility. Bi women in particular are portrayed as hypersexual, untrustworthy and incapable of staying committed in monogamous relationships. Bisexuality is also often portrayed as a transitional phase to being gay or lesbian, or a performance for the gaze of straight men. Bisexual people have combatted the invisibility by launching hashtags such as #BiTwitter to showcase the diversity of the bisexual community – yet even in that hashtag, bisexual people of colour are few and far between. In response, the hashtag #BlackBiBeauty was created to centre Black bisexual people and their experiences navigating both biphobia and racism within the LGBTQ+ community.[11] We need more spaces and opportunities for bisexual people of colour to amplify our unique experiences.

Bisexual people of colour are tasked with navigating both racism and biphobia in many LGBTQ+ spaces – spaces that are supposed to be safe for us to unapologetically exist. We are underrepresented, understudied, underfunded, and undervalued, yet we are critical to the success of the larger LGBTQ+ movement, and that's not okay. The B in LGBTQ+ isn't silent, and neither am I.

honouree lesbian:
it's a straight man's world

by Adam Reilly

I THINK THE lack of open discussion around the topic of sexuality in many of our childhoods has added to much of the uncertainty people face when contemplating their own identities. Personally, I was raised in a liberal house where it didn't really matter what or who you were, as long as you were a decent human being. Yet, there was still a huge lack of conversation around the matter, which probably added to the many years it has taken me to accept my own identity.

I must have been eleven or twelve before I even learned what the term 'lesbian' meant. For a lot of my developing years, I thought that it was only men who could be attracted to the same sex. This was purely because I had not been aware that there was a word used to label gay women. I think I first learned the word lesbian from *The Simpsons*, and it completely changed the way young Adam viewed the world. I also remember my parents then telling me not to use that word. This was not out of hate or bigotry, but probably because they thought they were protecting their child from a more complicated world. Nevertheless, I can fondly recall swinging from the banisters of my childhood home shouting out 'Dad, you're a lesbian!' before scurrying back into my bed, thrilled with my newly added vocabulary. I truly believe those moments of flying around the house, past my bedtime, calling everyone and everything a lesbian, was the start of my sexual awakening.

2004 was really The Year of the Lesbian for me and what a fantastic year, but I knew that I could never actually be a part of the lesbian club, and that was a hard pill to swallow for a ten-year-old. It did, however, give me a desire to go find my own tribe – even if that meant my younger self would have to hang up his lesbian cap for the last time. I wasn't ready to ask myself if I was gay, even though that would surely have been the next natural step from being an honouree lesbian. I can't remember exactly when I first learned what bisexuality means, or anything about who could be bisexual. So, for many of my crucial developmental years, I thought you were either straight, gay or a lesbian and that was it.

I recall the way the adults in my life spoke about sexuality when I was a child and how I would hold onto certain passing comments. Those comments would linger into my young adult years for a long time. Now, as an adult myself, I think it is so important for us to think about the way we speak to children about sexuality during their formative years. From my own childhood, even though I knew that neither of my parents particularly cared what I identified as, from their speech I still knew that one outcome would be far more desirable to them than the other. I think parents oftentimes will push heterosexuality onto their children, not out of malice, but more so out of a want for their children to fit within the boundaries of normal society and not have to deal with the added struggles that an LGBTQ+ person must grow up with. I can understand parents trying to protect their children, but this protection can have such adverse effects on children who are trying to understand themselves in later years.

Because I never had an in-depth explanation, for a big part of my teens I thought bisexual people were either gay men or lesbian women who weren't willing to accept themselves for who they truly were, and during those years this became how I viewed myself. I saw bisexuality as a segue into acceptance, but also as a shield to use against society. Let's be honest, even modern society isn't a great place to be different, so I could completely understand why some people would want to label themselves as bisexual. To me, at the time, it was somewhere in the middle between heterosexuality and 'full-on' gay identity.

Some years later, when I was around 19 years of age, I was starting to finally accept myself as a gay man. Then I started having 'the dreams'. Don't worry, the dreams weren't at all menacing, I just tend to flare towards the dramatic. I was having erotic dreams about women to the point of orgasm (which I need not say was more than confusing to someone like me, who tread carefully on the narrow line of sexual identity). The feeling of ecstasy that came with those orgasms was like a calamity washing through the halls of my mind and through the labyrinth where I kept my sexuality incarcerated.

My black and white vision of sexuality started to become tinted more and more with colour, and as I became surer of myself, I knew sexuality was so much more fluid than I could ever have understood in my younger years. As a young adult,

I began to see that sexuality wasn't like picking out paint colours from a chart; instead it should be viewed through a kaleidoscope to fully appreciate the diversity of human sexuality. I started to learn not to limit myself to restrictive labels and instead found myself viewing bisexuality as the perfect term to encompass all my own feelings about a fluid sexuality.

I'm still learning that finding yourself doesn't necessarily equate to those around you finding you too. I remember a group of my closest and oldest friends got together for a dinner celebrating one of their birthdays. I arrived a few minutes late to the dinner, as one does when wanting to make an entrance. As I sat down one of my oldest friends, Glenn, turned to me and said, 'Alright lad, or girl or whatever you want to be called' ('Alright' is an Irish slang term for hello). Glenn is very dear to my heart and not only is he a brilliant creative, but he is a very open-minded individual. He always has been. I know he didn't mean any ill intent with his words – it was, after all, just a simple greeting. However, it showed me that just because I identify as bisexual, I am viewed as less of a man, as if there were some sort of link between sexual orientation and gender. Glenn's simple greeting was an eye-opening moment for me because it showed me that even the friends I grew up with didn't really see me as a 'proper' guy because of my sexual identity. I guess it must link back to some sort of hypermasculinity complex, and if my friends were to treat a bisexual man as their equal, then it would be a threat upon their own sexuality and identity.

My circle of friends consists of about 90% heterosexual men, and being around these boys for so many years has made me aware that heterosexual culture can often be full of double standards. I've noticed that straight males treat their LGBTQ+ friends in the same way they treat straight women.

For example, I have spent the last decade watching my friends giving each other a pat on the back every time one of them hooks up with a girl, but when I share about hooking up with a guy, suddenly the lads disband the male hetero pride parade because my sex life is not something to be celebrated. In my experience, the sexual conquests of LGBTQ+ men and straight women are viewed as something to be kept private rather than celebrated, because male hetero culture doesn't want to concern itself with the sexual activities of anyone that doesn't fall under its narrow perception of what sexual activity should be.

I think when I was younger, I felt isolated from my friends because I knew that there were some differences they would rather not discuss, so instead I went out in search of my tribe. I never found it. But I think what I was searching for for all those years was already around me, and not some foreign concept. While things aren't always easy, I know that integration is the only way forward. I have not have found a group of LGBTQ+ people that I can turn to when I want to talk about things that fall outside the comfort zone of your average straight male (which admittedly can be a lonely place at times) but I never really held any ill will towards my straight male friends; after all their attitudes were just the result of their upbringing and society. My friends are growing and learning with me every day, and now I can say that those straight boys have been my tribe all along. It just takes time.

I can't express in words how important it is for the parents of straight children, especially boys, to speak freely about sexuality from a young age. The world we live in is run by the straight white male and has been for some time. The straight white male sets the agenda, and his value and belief systems have such a massive impact on society. I implore parents and guardians to speak openly not only about sexuality but about race, religion, gender, and beyond. Those early years are so crucial in how we go on to view the world, and ultimately how the straight white male will go on to see the world. Remember nobody is born with prejudice; if you are reading this, then you have the power to start the change.

jigsaw:
on bisexual representation in lgbtq+ history

by Mel Reeve

FROM AN EARLY age, I have been drawn to history and literature. I have always wanted to know everything I can about the past because it helps me understand how the world works, but I didn't always have access to resources that would help me research the history of my own identity – something I desperately craved. I remember as a child asking an adult why I liked a friend of mine (who happened to be a girl) so much; she said to me *maybe you have a crush on her*. I didn't really understand what that meant, but felt a prickling sense of shame that I had somehow crossed a line by voicing something better left unspoken. It was the first time I had asked someone about what it meant to have those feelings, and the only time for many years to come; instead, I lived with this secret that I couldn't even name. It would be a long time until I had the vocabulary to express my sexuality, and longer still before I had the chance to explore the history of my identity and of the LGBTQ+ community.

The histories of LGBTQ+ people are often not considered acceptable or even important enough to be included in education. Historical figures with same-sex partners or in relationships that do not conform to the heterosexual, patriarchal expectation often have that part of their lives reduced or erased completely from the academic narrative. This kind of revisionism is particularly easy to do with bisexual people because their relationships which do not conform to patriarchal norms of heterosexuality can be intentionally concealed or forgotten.

There is a movement to improve this representation. The work of historians, archivists, researchers, institutions, and individuals with an interest in preserving and promoting the experiences of LGBTQ+ people through history is redressing the balance. But the erasure of non-heterosexual relationships and bisexuality in particular still continues. In part this is because modern, Western definitions of sexuality and gender are a relatively new phenomenon. This makes the process of understanding how people would have identified outside of the current framework very difficult to comprehend. It is also important to acknowledge that some relationships which were historically perceived as same-sex will have involved transgender or non-binary people, but knowing how individuals would have defined themselves (especially when the terms we use are contemporary, Western definitions) is complicated. For this reason, in this essay I will refer to relationships in general between LGBTQ+ people as queer, rather than same-sex. However, just because the words might be different or it is harder to define a relationship or an individual's identity does not make recognising the legacy of the modern LGBTQ+ community any less important. We cannot allow the potential complexity of discussing this topic to reduce its importance and truth.

I grew up in the rural south-west of England in a very small community, at a time when the internet was just becoming widespread. I was well into primary school before Section 28 (which prohibited the so-called 'promotion' of homosexuality in schools) was finally repealed. It is perhaps not surprising then that I don't remember having any role models from the LGBTQ+ community (especially ones that looked or felt like me) until I was well into my teenage years. Even then their lives seemed so far away from my experiences.

I certainly didn't have any awareness of the rich history of the LGBTQ+ community – I was an anxious bisexual teenager, genuinely afraid that I was the first person ever to have these feelings and trying desperately to understand in particular what it means to be in this in-between space as a bisexual person. I remember my best friend recommending me *Sugar Rush*, a Channel 4 drama about two school girls – one of whom is gay. It was a pivotal moment for me, seeing representation of attraction and affection between women. But parts of *Sugar Rush* also enforced the stereotype of gay women as predatory. I remember getting changed for PE, terrified to look up from the floor in case the other girls could see in my eyes that I was different, genuinely believing that there was something deviant about me; that I was perverted just for existing. This feeling didn't start to dissipate for a really long time, and still materialises occasionally.

I began to discover more LGBTQ+ history when I went to university, where I studied English. But even then, when analysing texts, we were taught to be wary of forcing our contemporary definitions of identity onto characters or relationships with potentially LGBTQ+ readings. This is an important part of understanding historical queer relationships, but ultimately it seemed to result in a silencing of any discussion or exploration of the vibrant LGBTQ+ heritage that I know exists in our literature and histories. Queer relationships have existed as far back as you can look; applying modern labels in an attempt to define and acknowledge them *is* complicated, but the difficulty of getting that nuance right shouldn't stop us from exploring and celebrating them.

Take Shakespeare for example; the works he wrote which explored (what we would now understand as) queer relationships have been sanitised, but we know Shakespeare wrote about having romantic feelings for other men, as well as women. One of his most famous poems, Sonnet 18 (perhaps better known for its opening lines, '*Shall I compare thee to a summer's day? Thou art more lovely and more temperate*' ...) is a good example of this, because when read in context of the whole collection it becomes clear the narrator is addressing a man. This was only mentioned in my studies as a passing joke, or explained away under theory and arguments that it was just a 'literary exercise' to write beautiful, passionate love poetry about men, rather than an expression of any genuine feeling.

Of course, writers can create works from the perspectives of fictional narrators rather than their own, but it raises a question for me as to why there is not also space to just take this type of work at face value, as we do when Shakespeare's works address women or present heterosexual relationships. Going as far back as the 17th century there is a legacy of Shakespeare's works that have queer themes (like this poem) being taken out of context to erase that element – an issue which clearly still continues today. Because of this tradition of silencing and erasing identities, I have had to seek representations out for myself. I have had to look for writing and art by people with my experiences, and unlearn this inclination to minimise queer readings.

Despite the English degree, I only recently read Radclyffe Hall's *The Well of Loneliness* for the first time. It is written from the perspective of a lesbian narrator called Stephen who has relationships with several women (although Stephen's character can also be read as a transgender man). I was deeply moved when I read this book because it was the style of writing I had loved so much as a young teenager, and in addition, it represented feelings for which I previously had no cultural or historical reference point. *The Well of Loneliness* is not a happy or especially positive example of a queer relationship or experience, but it showed me how we must value and promote our histories. Seeing historical representation of feelings that had made me feel isolated and alone reminded me that I am part of a legacy of LGBTQ+ people. Reading just one book like that when I was younger and having a sincere analysis form part of my education would certainly have given me some comfort, not to mention a starting point to explore and understand myself further.

Another key moment for me was discovering Virginia Woolf's own bisexuality. Seeing the relationship she had with Vita Sackville-West was particularly important. They exchanged passionate, moving love letters – Sackville-West at one point writing 'I am reduced to a thing that wants Virginia'.[1] Discovering this made me realise how the bisexual themes in Woolf's writing were not explored as fully as they should have been in my education, and how much it would have meant to me to have discovered this at a younger age. For example, the kiss between Clarissa Dalloway and Sally

Seton in *Mrs Dalloway* is Clarissa's fondest memory. This gets reduced to an expression of her desire for freedom; it is explored as a literary device or an opportunity for character development, rather than as a queer relationship.

Another of my favourite writers is Sappho, the archaic Greek poet. Her very name has become short-hand for passionate relationships between women and her home, the Isle of Lesbos, gave us the word lesbian – but it was only recently that I discovered she also wrote love poetry about men. I am not a Greek scholar; her poetry is only accessible to me in translation and is infamously made up of fragments. As with Shakespeare, there is a wealth of academic debate about the difficulty of defining her sexuality. The ultimate answer is that we can never know for sure or hope to fully understand, from a modern perspective, how she saw herself. But for me, this does not diminish how important and moving it is to know that even that far back there existed someone with feelings and an identity which reflected mine.

There is also so much to be discovered from looking at how Sappho has been treated historically; a 2nd-century Christian writer named Tatian called her (exact wording depending on the translation you read) 'a whore who sang about her own licentiousness'.[2] Sappho's life and works were subjected to a smear campaign because of the content of her writing. After Tatian's words, there were more revisionist attempts made by historians to try to make her palatable again, which forced her into contemporary perceptions of acceptability. A German scholar wrote in the 1800s that Fragment 31 showed 'nothing but a friendly affection'[3] (perhaps the original 'gals just being pals' erasure).

Sappho is complicated, but the fact that I can only enjoy her work in fragments, through the lens of translation, means that instead of trying to decide how she really would have defined herself, I can simply read ancient writing about emotions and experiences that I too understand. Fundamentally, this is the value of these works – we do not have to know why an author wrote about queer relationships, or how they defined themselves, to enjoy and have access to our histories through their work. This is especially important to bisexuals because there is a real perception that bisexuality is somehow new, and that because of that we do not have the same right to a sense of historical culture. For example, the Instagram account @h_e_r_s_t_o_r_y, which shares 'historic lesbian imagery 1800s-1999s' recently shared an image of a magazine from 1995 with the headline 'Bisexuality: Not Gay. Not Straight. A New Sexual Identity Emerges'.

I recently read an article in *The Guardian* which talked about how important it is to preserve LGBTQ+ spaces like Pride from becoming sanitised and palatable for the heterosexual world, except it didn't talk about all LGBTQ+ people – it only made repeated reference to 'lesbians and gay men'.[4] As I was reading, I started to wonder if that was accidental or intentional, but it soon became clear. The only specific mention of bisexuals was used to suggest that having them in queer spaces dilutes the validity and importance of these spaces.

It is so disappointing to still see this attitude; bisexual people are still being told we do not have a legacy and history as part of this community, and that we somehow dilute the validity of LGBTQ+ spaces by existing in them. Bisexual people should be aware of the privilege we can have and act accordingly in LGBTQ+ spaces, but it is also important to remember that we do not have the feeling of safety or belonging that heterosexual people get in their spaces (i.e. everywhere else). We have been an integral part of this community the whole time; just one example being Brenda Howard, who was a key figure in the genesis of Pride. Howard coordinated a march to commemorate the first anniversary of the Stonewall riots – all while married to a man. When we talk only of 'lesbian and gay' history, I can't help but think of the bisexual people that have been erased because of the inability – from parts of the LGBTQ+ community as well as from many heterosexual people – to recognise that bisexual identity has a history and legacy. Because of this erasure, bi history is inevitably interlinked with the histories of lesbian and gay people. Promoting the latter is very important, but we should remember and acknowledge that bisexual people existed in those histories too.

The Guardian's article is just one example of modern biphobia from within the LGBTQ+ community, and it's all the sadder to me because I know how much more the community is capable of when we all stand in support of each other. Many bisexuals do have privilege, but we also understand the struggles and difficulties that form a sad but often inevitable part of queer experiences. That privilege comes at its own cost too; bisexual people are more at risk of intimate partner violence, suicide, and poverty. Ineke Mushovic, executive director of the Movement Advancement Project, which published the report evidencing these facts, describes some of the potential causes of this phenomenon:

> *Despite comprising the largest population within the LGBT community, bisexual people are among the most invisible... The failure to account for bisexual lives and experiences compounds a lack of social support and keeps bisexual people in the closet.*[5]

So, while my current relationship fits a definition that gives me greater freedom than is afforded to those in visibly LGBTQ+ relationships, and I firmly acknowledge that and work to ensure I am not minimising more marginalised voices, I am still a part of this community. This is because in my heart I will always be that frightened child who thinks they are the only person in the world who feels this way. I will always be the teenager that gets called a dyke on the way home from school and thinks how do they know. I will always be the adult sat in a room of other LGBTQ+ people who is made to feel that this space is not for them, but has nowhere else to look for a sense of community. I treasure my friendships with other LGBTQ+ people deeply, but my friendships with other bi people are particularly precious, because they understand this dichotomy of never being quite enough of either culture.

I've always known there was something different about me. That part was never confusing – a word so often used to minimise and reduce bisexual people and our experiences. It was just how everyone else treated me and expected me to behave that was confusing. There is no singular definition of any LGBTQ+ identity, and you do not have to suffer to have a claim to your sexuality or gender – though suffering is unfortunately an experience we almost all have in common. You do not have to prove your identity to anyone, and your experiences and struggles do not create the fundamental fact of it.

When I was young I wished so desperately that I would wake up and be straight, and after that I briefly started to wish I was a lesbian because I felt like an interloper, laying claim to a heritage and history that did not belong to me. Now I know I am part of a rich history of bisexual people: the pieces of our jigsaw exist, it's just that sometimes it's up to us to put them together. We have always been there – lost in either side of history, almost always hidden away as straight or gay – but we were there and we are here now, even if you don't see us.

fml: fix my life

by Joseph Guthrie

THE NIGHT AIR up on that fourteen-storey building was eerily comforting. I stood atop a fire escape balcony looking hundreds of feet down to where I'd ascended from, tear ducts welling up not from a sense of sadness but purely from the brisk wind whipping my itchy eyes. I wanted to cry. I desperately wanted to break down into a blubbering, hysterical mess instead of deciding to take just one step forward.

One step and it'll all be over. No more pain. No more depression. No more pain. There'll be no more feeling a sense of abject worthlessness. No more pain.

No more.

I raised my head toward the skyline of the city of my birth. The Old Smoke. The Great Wen. Londinium. Immediately a flash of anger flooded my body, goosebumps prickling my weathered skin. I started to feel faint and then... then came the voice. My voice. 'Jump, you pussy.' I felt compelled to look down, so I did. I imagine it was because my sense of sound – my sonar, if you will – was so hypersensitive, I didn't need to guess where the voice came from. It was my voice, after all. No sooner had I gazed upon the ground than I saw a ravaged, bloodied version of me. It was me as if I had already jumped. *This is it*, I thought. *This is what madness is. I've fucking lost my mind. I... I can't be fucking seeing this shit!* I looked away at the same time as I felt something in the pit of my gut sharply lurch upward toward my chest cavity. Dry heaving? No, no. I did not feel *that* physically ill, but the mirage of me standing and looking up, repeatedly saying 'Jump, you pussy. Jump, you pussy' wouldn't go away. He wouldn't – I wouldn't, instead, say anything else. Just egged me on to jump. I'm so... persistent. *How do you turn your goddamn brain off?!* I'm feeling thirstier by the second and my voice is getting more menacing in tone. I'm terrified to look down again, but I must. I must double check I'm not losing my sanity here.

It's not me I'm staring at anymore. It looks a lot like me. No, it's my father, and he looks just like he did the night he beat the shit out of me; wearing that same work uniform for the security installation firm where he once worked. It's happening *again*. Every single time I have a suicidal episode, I continually go back to that night. That awful, awful night. So, what if I brought a report card home with bad marks on it? Why react like this? Why treat me this way? Why clasp your hands around my neck? Why can't I breathe? Why does everything hurt so bad? Why is everything going white? Why Dad? Why?

I climbed back over the railing and backed away from the edge. I forced myself to walk right back down the fire escape steps that I had previously ascended for what I thought would be a one-way journey. I went back inside my office building, zombified and completely numb. My eyes were starting to glaze over, having stared at the monitoring software on my computer screen for so long. So I lifted my head up, only to see the same fire escape again. I quickly looked back at the screen, and then I looked to my left, only to see the charred shell of Grenfell Tower in full panoramic view on the London horizon line. I then excused myself once more and went down to the breakout room. *Sleep*, I thought. *Just sleep now. Just relax. Sleep.*

Unless you're Christopher Nolan, telling any story with a fractured, idiosyncratic narrative won't automatically get you the kind of plaudits he got when *Memento* released to critical acclaim in 2000, but that's pretty much what my life has been like: a fractured, idiosyncratic, tangled web of anecdotes and anti-depressants. I find myself flashing back to moments like the aforementioned; ones synonymous with the feeling I get whenever I embrace the genuine possibility that today is going to be my last. Inextricably linked with the vivid and sometimes lucid recollection of traumatic moments from days gone by were all the things about who I am as a human being. Matters that I thought I was content keeping hidden away from plain view were eroding away at my soul and exacerbating a deep, clinical depression. To be Joseph Guthrie is to be a Black, pansexual, depressive dork; trapped inside your twisted mind, frantically trying to get out and by the time the opening credits to the latest suicidal episode have finished rolling, you realise you're never indeed escaping. My mind is akin to a demoralising MC Esher sketch: caught in an infinite looping of self-mutilation, suicidal ideation, and unresolved trauma from experiences past that continue to haunt me like some vengeful spectre.

I grew up convinced that I was the only person going through this. There was no one I could relate to, categorically not in my immediate or extended family. I knew of no one else in the numerous communities I had inhabited over the years apart from a few gay men, the odd trans woman, and some lesbians that could talk me through what life would be like as a bisexual/pansexual cis male. If anything, some of them would make trite jokes about how bi people didn't exist and that we're just 'greedy', depraved, hypersexual perverts that love nothing more than to fuck anyone willing and without attachment. My sexuality, like my mental illness, was constantly bombarded with hot take after radioactive, speculative, and frankly unhelpful hot take. Between the other residents of the LGBTQ+ community making it seem bisexuality 'didn't exist' and the cis heterosexual folks making bi men out to be harbingers of doom, destruction, and disease, the safest place for me was incidentally the place that was killing me: inside the closet. I leant heavily on the tenet of 'It's no one's business who I sleep with apart from whom I'm sleeping with'. When asked 'What am I?' I relied on vague answers tantamount to 'I'm just me.' Sometimes, to throw people off my scent, I'd straight up lie about my sexuality. 'Nah, I'm straight,' I'd say, going on years later to start preambles to my rants or observations with 'As a cis hetero man', knowing full well that I'd just had sex with another cute guy the night before.

No one told me bisexual Black men experienced depression and anxiety at higher rates than the rest of the general populace,[1] and as an avid reader, I never found any reading material explaining what studies had already confirmed. No one told me that discrimination and harassment based on both racism and homophobia doubly contribute to the depression and anxiety bisexual Black men live and struggle with. No one told me bisexual men are more likely to conceal their sexual orientation and less likely to disclose their sexuality than gay men.[2] No one told me bisexual Black men were more likely to self-harm.[3] No one – not even those closest to me, who care about me profoundly – pointed me in the direction of any of these resources. What folks did tell me was that my mental illness was all in my head, completely contradicting the diagnoses from the doctors, psychiatrists, and therapists that my mother brought me to. What folks did tell me was that bisexuality was a myth, a unicorn; that bi people were 'confused' because we didn't fit into the rigid sexual dichotomy that we are all forced into.

I know it seems a bit annoying of me to keep mentioning depression and bisexuality in the same breath, but don't miss the point I'm trying to make here: poor mental health and living life as a closeted bi/pan Black man are inextricably linked. It is a treacherous tightrope walk because as society moves to ostracise you for what they can see in the colour of your skin, society is also waging war against you for what they fear and wilfully misunderstand regarding your sexuality. To be Black and part of the LGBTQ+ demographic is the physical manifestation of the turn of phrase 'Can't win for losing'. To be Black and bisexual/pansexual, precisely, is to intimately know what life is like from the intersection of erasure and discrimination. On the one hand, you're made out by non-Black people to be some subhuman, innately criminal monstrosity. On the other hand, you're made to feel like an imposter because people refuse to accept something as perfectly axiomatic as being sexually attracted to and capable of forming intimate, romantic relationships with people regardless of gender or sex.

No one told me my life would be anything like this, and that's why I'm speaking to you, whether you want to listen or not.

Life in the closet or 'on the down low' is a life fraught with immense pressure to hide a massive part of your humanity. It is not a comfortable existence at all, even though everything appears to be just fine on the surface. I handled my struggle with this almost identically as I did my battle with depression over the years. As time went by, I became increasingly jaded with the prospect of seeking any assistance at all; presuming I'd hear the same delegitimising rubbish I'd heard before. Nevertheless, my very existence was under threat from forces seen and unseen, and while I was surrounded by people who tried their best to help me, they were just as clueless as I was in obtaining effective counsel. For years, I felt like an outsider no matter where I turned, and it didn't matter where I sought sanctuary because it was never safe enough for me to pull back the invisibility cloak I had draped over a significant part of who I am as a human being. The desire to liberate myself intensified, but the fear of being alienated by the few people I truly trusted in this world was utterly crippling. It's all well and good saying you don't give a fuck what anyone thinks of you, but the proof in the pudding is in the eating, and many of us just don't have the appetite for it.

Once the dead weight of 2016 was shed, and 2017 rolled in, I would cross paths with someone who would not only change my life forever, but in whom I found someone that I could sincerely relate to. Standing at five feet five inches tall with a booming voice and a bombastic personality, Meredith quote tweeted me about a band we mutually loved. That conversation went from the timeline into the direct messages and from there, our exchange moved to FaceTime. I was instantly taken by her laugh, her smile, and it was utterly breath-taking how much we had in common. Imagine it: here are two strangers on two different sides of the Atlantic Ocean having the time of their lives just... talking to one another. I couldn't recall a time when an eight-hour conversation felt like eight minutes. Just speaking to her wholly melted away any issues I knew I had to contend with once we disconnected. It was when she mentioned her ex-wife that I realised all this time, I had been looking in the wrong place for a kindred spirit to talk to about bisexuality and all of the unique foibles that come along with that part of a bi/pan person's self-discovery.

Coming out to my previous partners made me feel like I disgusted them by telling them what they never knew, but telling Meredith was as natural as breathing or walking. I didn't have to think about it. I knew I could trust her. Up to that moment, I had only ever divulged that information to people I thought I could confide in, or at the very least to whomever I thought wasn't a threat. Looking back on it, the bond that I forged with Meredith had to be of divine conception. There's no way you find this kind of camaraderie with someone on a social media application. Sure, you hear the stories, but the chances of it happening to someone like me were so slim, they might as well be non-existent. We became fast friends... and in the midst of all of the individual and collective chaos in our lives, we found love. I'll never forget when she called me one morning and confessed to me that she had done something that was intended to be a surprise. She had spent money she didn't really have to buy a plane ticket to London from where she was based in Philidelphia. When she sent a screenshot of her boarding pass as proof, my first words were 'WHAT DID YOU DO?!' She laughed, as did I. I don't think I'll ever run up a flight of stairs as fast as I did the morning she arrived in London

Heathrow. The initial embrace confirmed what I had previously been dismissive about: I fell in love with Meredith. She quickly became and still is my best friend. By merely existing, she showed me how to be unapologetic about carrying yourself and who you are at your core. She had been 'out' for about as long as I had been 'in the closet'. When I told her that I wasn't exactly 'out', she responded with encouragement and compassion. There was no pressure placed on me. She said to me with a voice like hushed bells, 'When you're ready, dude. When you're ready, you'll take that step'.

That all-consuming desire to liberate myself and finally come out to the world reached a level of fervour that would make the fires of hell feel like a sauna session. I'd had enough. *It will happen this year.* No advance warnings to my mother, brothers, and sisters. I don't need their approval or blessing, anyway. This is who I am, and like the glorious melanin adorning my skin, my sexuality is axiomatic. I remember saying to my friends in our WhatsApp group that I'd use Bisexual Awareness Week as the perfect milieu for such an undertaking, but after my suicidal episode in June, I knew I couldn't wait any longer. I knew what I had to do. So the moment Pride in London got underway, I took to my platforms on social media and did it. I told my entire truth.

I am Bisexual. I am Pansexual.

And almost immediately after completing the thread on Twitter and hitting 'Post' on Facebook, the shackles loosened, and the chains fell at my feet. Tears of relief and joy streamed down my face. The phone rang. I answered, and the first words I heard were from a familiar source; the tone of voice like hushed bells.

'Baby, I'm so proud of you,' Meredith gushed.

I saved myself from myself. I had just resolved one of the most significant and most protracted internal conflicts that I had going. In other words, coming out not only saved my life. It gave me a sense of renewed purpose, and that's part of the reason why you're reading this now. Chances are you're not Black. Chances are you're not bisexual or pansexual. Chances are you're not a cisgendered man. If you aren't any or only some of these things, then I humbly thank you for taking the time to read these scribings, and I hope my experience has imparted something of significant use to you going forward.

However, if you are a Black, bisexual/pansexual man – cisgender or transgender – then know this: you are beautiful. The world needs you. *You* need to be the best you possible. I know it seems like there's not one drop of energy or courage left in the tank right now, but I need you to dig deep and find your last reserve if need be. The world wilfully misunderstands our existence, but that doesn't give them the right to erase us, because it was never a right of theirs in the first place. For this reason and more, we must stand. Stand and be as conspicuous as possible. Stand and show your true self.

When you're ready, dudes. When you're ready, you'll take that first step.

revelations
on sex, sexuality, and religion

by Dany Carter

As SHORT A time ago as 2009 the idea of bisexuality left me queasy, uncomfortable at the thought of a new aberrance whose motives and mechanics I didn't understand. I remember reading the MySpace profile of a new friend, seeing that surprise, lurking label – bi – and feeling a rush of unsettled sadness, as if I'd discovered an unforeseen, unfortunate secret about someone I was coming to be fond of. The urge to love and to be kind superseded, and months later, sitting at coffee with the same friend who now told me she was gay, I said nothing unsupportive, no critique moral or social, no probing questions, just listened. In retrospect, my silence may have spoken volumes, but I tried to hide the subtle battle waging internally.

That evening I journaled out part of the skirmish: my first lesbian friend, and the inner conflict I felt about how to react.

I remember this entry because I've read it over a few times since then. The part that bothered me, that day, was that *it didn't bother me*. At heart I didn't really mind if she was gay; it was new, it was something to get used to, but I didn't actually disapprove. The conflict came because I felt that I should: because according to the worldview I then still professed to espouse, I *should* think it was wrong. That cognitive dissonance was the rub.

I have a complex relationship with religion: I don't hate it. Sometimes when my liberal friends rail against its evils, it even hurts me. It hurts me because God, and Christianity – though not the church institution per se – were an integral part of my life for so long, and still matter deeply to many people I love. I hold two parts in suspension now: the one that cannot honestly worship or participate in religious community anymore, who sees the many flaws of the social philosophies that tend to accompany mainline Christianity. But there's another part of me that felt love there, that felt meaning; who still believes we are more than just bodies living purposeless lives, who still prays sometimes when she is frightened or grieving. I'm very aware of the contradictions. I doubt that I'll ever fully solve them. I think that once something has grown so deep inside you, a part of it will always linger.

But even if I'm some vague theistic agnostic, I stopped professing Christianity years ago, after a logical and emotional attrition of almost a decade. I couldn't wholeheartedly say I wanted to devote my life to this. I couldn't honestly agree to the ideas and philosophies that run so deeply in Christian doctrine, so a pragmatic step of honesty with myself was to remove myself from active belief. And one of the points of contention – the cruxes which made me realise I did not ally with this doctrine – was sexuality.

As you've already likely gathered, I grew up believing that homosexuality was wrong – and even further, that sex of any kind should be saved for heterosexual marriage. My community was thankfully not as prudish or restrictive as some conservative circles; in fact, it was conditionally sex-positive, and sex life in a marriage was seen as a source of pleasure and intimacy, not merely procreation. However, the condition was there, as was the (willing) assumption in my teen years that I wouldn't be having sex any time soon. This led to a certain cavalier approach to sex education in a 'this will be relevant later' sense; I knew how babies were made, and the basic forms of birth control, but I had never so much as touched a condom. I didn't actually know what the clitoris was until I was 19, and words like 'orgasm' were semi-threatening outliers, floating on the edge of my understanding. They were uncomfortable because they both impugned how ignorant I was and smacked of the transgressive.

The mythic strictures around virginity and sexual purity espoused by conservative Christianity made any kind of physical intimacy outside of a committed relationship feel dangerous to me. Not because I didn't want it, but because I did and felt I shouldn't – much in same the way that I felt guilt for not having a problem with my friend's lesbianism. I was irredeemably logical within the philosophical framework I'd been taught: no picking and choosing and bending the rules. If I couldn't agree with the rules, I'd have to scrap the framework, which is eventually what I did. But years of sublimating sexual desire led to a deep difficulty approaching or bonding with men, and sex for its own sake was out of the question. Even after I had abandoned abstinence as a moral philosophy and felt open to the idea of sex, it loomed as a diaphanous cloud of unknowns, which as I got older began to feel like a hassle, and virginity became a habit rather than an intention. I remained a virgin until my mid-twenties when I entered my first relationship – a relationship with a woman.

How did someone who quailed at the notion of bisexuality, and who was so sexually repressed she felt guilty for even kissing a man, get to this point? It would be easier to say there was a series of revelations, but it wasn't that quick or that clear. It was a slow progression of allowing myself to acknowledge things that I deep down already knew.

Dismantling my outward homophobia was the easier part, thanks to formative time spent with lesbian, gay, genderqueer and trans friends. It's amazing how aversions and fears that we couch as instinctual are actually all a matter of exposure. I used to physically jolt at the thought of same-sex inter-course (*how strange and how wrong!*) and for a time I thought that this was my inner compass guiding me. Now, I share a healthy sex life with my girlfriend. Am I a different person? Have I lost my moral compass? No, because in reality those supposed instincts were merely custom and familiarity, and once I started to meet, talk with, laugh with, and understand LGBTQ+ people, their lives began to feel normal. I often forget that I am in a 'gay' relationship – partially because, try as I might, I still have some odd internalised disconnect from that term. But mostly because our relationship feels so natural to me that I don't think of it as something 'other', which culturally, homosexuality still sadly is.

My internalised homophobia – see the disconnect above – has taken much longer to unravel. Basic human sympathy which then grows into support of other people's lifestyle choices is one thing. Allowing *myself* to take part in that lifestyle is wholly another. Two or three years before I met my partner, I began to think of myself as 'probably bi' – I recognised that I had the capacity for attraction to women. But I didn't really expect it to ever happen, and saw myself ending up with a man. I felt that for me, sex with a woman must be experimentation, and therefore irresponsible toward the feelings of whatever woman it happened with. I sat on the side-lines and did not consider myself part of the LGBTQ+ community.

All religious and conservative upbringing aside, I felt I did not fit in with queer spaces because I simply was not queer enough. I was a cis woman who really liked men. I still often feel the same alienation, which I have come to realise is common to many bisexual people. I still like men, and speaking objectively, I'm attracted to them more often than to women. I appear quite traditionally feminine and pass automatically for straight. But I am not straight. And finally I had to approach that from a purely individual level – divorced from any group identification or allegiance or paradigm – to realise and embrace it. I had to follow what felt right *only for me*, without the guidelines of religion or the stereotypes of society interfering.

Later, after much internal hemming and hawing, I decided to enter a relationship with my girlfriend, and found it to be one of the most freeing, formative, and growth-inspiring decisions I've ever made. Besides bringing romance and well-being to my life, this relationship shed new light on another topic that religion taught me to fixate on: virginity. The culture of preserving sexual purity, and saving intercourse for heterosexual marriage, was psychologically stunting to me. It caused me to deny that I am (and always have been) a deeply sensual person, to dissociate from my physicality, to disempower myself, to make myself ashamed of pursuing pleasure for its own sake. The virginity complex made me small, frightened, and insecure. I don't claim it has this effect on everyone, but it did on me.

But now that I'm having sex with my girlfriend, the obsession with virginity seems all the more absurd. I have categorically never had a penis in my vagina – that much-feared and hallowed contact that separates the veil of virginity for so many cultures. Am I still a virgin then? I orgasm with my partner, but our intercourse doesn't even fulfil the traditional tenets of what constitutes sex in the community where I was raised. Where is the line when foreplay becomes sex? What constitutes loss of virginity? Merely stepping outside the bounds of a heteronormative enclosure makes us reassess what virginity really even is.

For so long, I felt that if I had sex, I was giving myself away. I was losing something, surrendering something to a man if he penetrated me, regardless of whether I enjoyed it or not. I mentally turned sex into a power play, an assertion of dominance, because I felt myself vulnerable and disempowered by the trappings of my own fabled virginity. Well, I don't like to lose, so I didn't play the game.

With all these complexes built up, perhaps it's unsurprising that I found healing in sex with a woman. It is equal, and loving, and giving, and that is what I needed. In experiencing the physical aspects of this relationship I also found myself reassessing my past life with less encumbered eyes: recognising that my attraction to women began far before I allowed myself to acknowledge it; realising how much the sexual creature of my early childhood was sublimated and shackled by shame through my young adult life.

Not everyone who has grown up religious has felt these strictures, surely; many will have adapted earlier, found a better way to reconcile their sexuality and sex drive with the philosophies of their faith. But I was always a serious child, and back then I did not deal in grey areas. I still find that in some ways I can't – which is perhaps why I had to remove myself from religion. In some part of my brain it is all or it is nothing.

I don't think that Christianity (or religion in general) is inherently negative, nor do I think it has to be sexist or homophobic. There are increasingly diverse biblical interpretations and subsequent nuances of belief in those respects. I can't even say that I wish I had grown up without my faith. That would be a lie. It was intrinsic to me, and retroactively removing it would be deeply wrong. But I can say that in my own experience, the rationales of my religion caused me to delay my own growth and stifle my identity for a principle that, on second look, was not even particularly important to me. I stunted my own sexual development; no one did it to me. No malevolent preachers or parents threatened me with hellfire for my sexual desires. The prison of my own mind was the culprit, holding me back from my sexual identity and the confidence and empowerment I could find in it.

The two prongs of my problem – heterosexuality and virginity – are not, I believe, essential to the practice of faith in any way. But they are all too often seized upon as some of the core fixations of conservative religion, and that is where the danger lies. In the end I had to step away from religion and its framework entirely in order to escape my philosophical and emotional self-sabotage.

So now, here I am, a very new bisexual, discovering sex and same-sex all at once, breaking not one but two rules of my faith-filled youth. When I think about God, as I am sometimes wont to do, I ask myself whether belief in him would require me to assume he disapproved. I think the answer is no. No, because what I have discovered is *self*: it is growth, love, the beauty of the individual, warm caresses and happiness, something that feels so right and simple and natural. God, if he observes, would find me a creation in motion: learning to celebrate both the value of my own self, and the unfathomable beauty that occurs when two human hearts come together. Perhaps he will not object to that.

references

Foreword

1. Barker, M., Richards, C., Jones, R., Bowes-Catton, H., Plowman, T., Yockney, J. & Morgan, M. (2012). *The bisexuality report: Bisexual inclusion in LGBT equality and diversity.* Milton Keynes: The Open University Centre for Citizenship, Identities and Governance.

Sexual Assault and Gender

1. Understanding Issues Facing Bisexual Americans. (n.d.). Retrieved from http://www.lgbtmap.org/file/understanding-issues-facing-bisexual-americans.pdf.
2. Grinberg, E., & Shoichet, C. E. (2016). Brock Turner released after 3 months in jail. Retrieved from http://

www.cnn.com/2016/09/02/us/brock-turner-release-jail/index.html.

3. College Fix Staff. (2016). USC study: Twenty-five percent of online comments in rape/sex assault articles 'blame the victim'. Retrieved from http://www.thecollegefix.com/post/28568/.

4. Chasmar, J. (2017). Mayim Bialik accused of 'victim blaming' in Harvey Weinstein op-ed. Retrieved from https://www.washingtontimes.com/news/2017/oct/16/mayim-bialik-accused-victim-blaming-harvey-weinste/.

5. Heldman, C. (2017). Bill Cosby's legal defense was a case study in rape culture. Retrieved from https://www.vox.com/first-person/2017/6/13/15793220/bill-cosby-trial-rape-culture.

6. Mahdawi, A. (2016). This is what rape culture looks like – in the words of Donald Trump. Retrieved from https://www.theguardian.com/us-news/2016/oct/15/donald-trump-words-what-rape-culture-looks-like.

7. RAINN. (n.d.). Retrieved from https://www.rainn.org/statistics/perpetrators-sexual-violence.

California Here I Come

1. Kornhaber, S. (2015). The Trope of the Evil Television Bisexual. Retrieved from https://www.theatlantic.com/entertainment/archive/2015/10/tvs-evil-bisexuals-still-live/412786.

Defining Terms

1. Lick, D. J., Durso, L. E., & Johnson, K. L. (2013). Minority stress and physical health among sexual minorities.

Perspectives on Psychological Science, 8 (5), 521–548.

2. Bowleg, L. (2012). The problem with the phrase women and minorities: intersectionality—an important theoretical framework for public health. *American Journal of Public Health*, 102 (7), 1267–1273.

3. Meyer, I. H. (2003). Prejudice, social stress, and mental health in lesbian, gay, and bisexual populations: conceptual issues and research evidence. *Psychological Bulletin*, 129 (5), 674.

'Not Like That, Like This'

1. Lowen, L. (2017). Abstinence Only Education and Sex Education in the U.S. Retrieved from https://www.thoughtco.com/abstinence-only-sex-education-3533767.

2. Guttmacher Institute. (2016). Sex and HIV Education. Retrieved from https://www.guttmacher.org/state-policy/explore/sex-and-hiv-education.

3. http://lgbthistorymonth.org.uk/wp-content/uploads/2014/05/1384014531S28Background.pdf

4. Bronski, M., Pellegrini, A., & Amico, M. (2013). *"You Can Tell Just By Looking" and 20 Other Myths about LGBT Life and People*. Boston: Beacon Press. Excerpted via http://www.slate.com/blogs/outward/2013/10/03/is_lesbian_sex_real_sex.html.

5. Ibid.

6. Ibid.

7. https://fetlife.com/ and http://www.vulvalpainsociety.org/vps/.

8. https://www.sh-womenstore.com/

Five Times I Felt Invisible as a Bisexual Fan

1. Lo, M. (2017). LGBTQ YA by the Numbers: 2015-16. Retrieved from https://www.malindalo.com/blog/2017/10/12/lgbtq-ya-by-the-numbers-2015-16.
2. https://fanlore.org/wiki/Headcanon.

A Place to 'B'

1. Percival, A. (2017). BBC Drama Bosses Admit The One Aspect Of LBGT+ Representation They Haven't Got Right. HuffPost UK. Retrieved from www.huffingtonpost.co.uk/entry/bbc-drama-bisexuality-bisexual-characters-soaps-eastenders_uk_5968af4ee4b03389bb169277.

Girlfriend Wanted

1. Ortberg, M. (2016). It's Complicated. Slate. Retrieved from http://www.slate.com/articles/life/dear_prudence/2016/02/dear_prudence_my_wife_insists_on_telling_men_she_s_bisexual.html

On Being Black and Bi-Furious

1. Flanders, Dobinson, and Logie (2015) and Johnson (2016) are good articles to look at for those interested in the intersections between bisexuality and mental health.
2. Bisexual researchers who have had an especially strong impact on me include Paula Rust, Shiri Eisner, and especially Robyn Ochs. I also identify with Och's definition of bisexuality as 'the potential to be attracted – romantically and/or sexually – to people of more than one sex and/or

gender, not necessarily at the same time, not necessarily in the same way, and not necessarily to the same degree.'

3. Duggan's *The New Homonormativity: The Sexual Politics of Neoliberalism* (2002) defines homonormativity as the ways that mainstream gay rights movements perpetuate and reinforce heteronormativity within LGBTQ+ spaces.

4. Roberts, Horne, & Hoyt (2015) offers great insight on bisexual people's experiences with navigating mono-sexism, and Hayfield, Clark & Halliwell (2014) focuses specifically on bisexual women's experiences with mono-sexism in both straight and lesbian communities.

5. Nathanson (2001) interviewed activists who were involved in the march, and clearly explains both sides. This is great for understanding the historical tensions between lesbian and bisexual women.

6. The exact quote is found on page 10 of the assessment, which can be found on the Bisexual Organizing Project's website under the "About" tab.

7. Additionally, the 2012 Bisexual Community Needs Assessment can also be found on the Bisexual Organizing Project's website under the "About" tab.

8. The percentage of LGBTQ+ adults in the United States as estimated by Gates (2011) does not include many LGBTQ+ people who are not out or who did not have access to the surveys.

9. Similarly to Gates' last study, the study with Kastanis (2013) also does not include Black LGBTQ+ people who are not out or did not have access to the surveys.

10. Based on previous reports by Funders for LGBTQ Issues, bisexual-specific funding has increased over the years. In 2009 and 2010, zero dollars were given to bisexual organisations. However, the bisexual community and the intersex community still get the least amount of funding.

11. Shoutout to TheAngryFangirl for launching this wonderful hashtag! Follow her on Twitter @TheAngryFangirl or visit her website theangryfangirl.com.

Burleson, W. E. (2012). Bisexual Community Needs Assessment. Bisexual Organizing Project, Minneapolis, Minnesota.

Duca, J. (1991). Needs Assessment of the Bisexual Community. Gay and Lesbian Community Action Council, Minneapolis, Minnesota.

Duggan, L. (2002). The new homonormativity: The sexual politics of neoliberalism. *Materializing democracy: Toward a revitalized cultural politics*, 175-94.

Flanders, C. E., Dobinson, C., & Logie, C. (2015). "I'm Never Really My Full Self": Young Bisexual Women's Perceptions of their Mental Health. *Journal of Bisexuality*, *15*(4), 454–480.

Gates, G. J. (2011). How many people are lesbian, gay, bisexual and transgender? Retrieved from https://escholarship.org/uc/item/09h684x2.pdf.

Hayfield, N., Clarke, V., & Halliwell, E. (2014). Bisexual women's understandings of social marginalisation: "The heterosexuals don"t understand us but nor do the lesbians'. *Feminism & Psychology*, *24*(3), 352–372.

Johnson, H. J. (2016). Bisexuality, Mental Health, and Media Representation. *Journal of Bisexuality*, *16*(3), 378–396.

Kan, L. M., Maulbeck, B. F., Wallace, A. (2017) 2015 Tracking Report: Lesbian, Gay, Bisexual, Transgender, and Queer Grantmaking by U.S. Foundations. Funders for LGBTQ Issues. Retrieved from https://www.lgbtfunders.org/wp-content/uploads/2017/05/2015_Tracking_Report.pdf.

Kastanis, A., & Gates, G. J. (2013). *LGBT African-Americans and African-American same-sex couples*. Williams Institute, UCLA School of Law.

Nathanson, J. (2001). Pride and Politics: Revisiting the Northampton Pride March, 1989-1993. Journal of Bisexuality, 2(2–3), 143–161.

Roberts, T. S., Horne, S. G., & Hoyt, W. T. (2015). Between a Gay and a Straight Place: Bisexual Individuals' Experiences with Monosexism. Journal of Bisexuality, 15(4), 554–569.

Jigsaw

1. Jones, J. (2016). The Steamy Love Letters of Virginia Woolf and Vita Sackville-West (1925-1929). Retrieved from http://www.openculture.com/2016/07/the-steamy-love-letters-of-virginia-woolf-and-vita-sackville-west-1925-1929.html.

2. Chrystal, P. (2017). Women in Ancient Greece. Fonthill Media.

3. Most, G. W. (1995). Reflecting Sappho. *Bulletin of the Institute of Classical Studies*, 40.

4. Hensher, P. (2017). How the straight majority still silences gay people. Retrieved from https://amp.theguardian.com/commentisfree/2017/jul/21/straight-majority-silences-gay-people-lesbians-pride.

5. Movement Advancement Project. (2014). New Report Details High Rates of Violence, Discrimination Toward Bisexual People. Retrieved from http://www.lgbtmap.org/news/understanding-issues-facing-bisexual-americans-release.

FML: Fix My Life

1. Sutton, A. (2011). Prejudice Linked to Depression, Anxiety in Gay and Bisexual Black Men. Retreived from http://www.cfah.org/hbns/2011/prejudice-linked-to-depression-anxiety-in-gay-and-bisexual-black-men.
2. Columbia University. (2013). Bisexual Men on the "Down Low" Run Risk for Poor Mental Health. Retrieved from https://www.mailman.columbia.edu/public-health-now/news/bisexual-men-down-low-run-risk-poor-mental-health.
3. Pebody, R. (2016). Poor mental health more commonly experienced by gay and bisexual men who are younger, poorer, less educated or black. Retrieved from https://www.aidsmap.com/Poor-mental-health-more-commonly-experienced-by-gay-and-bisexual-men-who-are-younger-poorer-less-educated-or-black/page/3057707/.

special thanks

THIS BOOK WAS made possible thanks to each and every one of our 200+ donors on Kickstarter. But a particular few people showed extra generosity by pledging to our highest reward tier, and we would like the extend them a special thank you. We would also like to thank those among our friends and professional peers who offered up their support and talent while we worked on the project. The following humans are absolute stars:

Anonymous Donor
Aisling McGing
Allison Lemley
Beth Brown
Cate Reed
Christina Sund

C Nickodemus
Collin Knopp-Schwyn
Emily Horgan
Eoghan Scott
Gerry Desmond
Gordon and Marian MacLean
Heather McDaid and Laura Jones
Jonny Gallant
John O'Connor
K Garthoff
Kirstyn Smith
Laura Hussey
Laura Ní Chíosain
Michael McTernan
Monica Pirani
Neasa O'Sullivan
Rebecca Bonallie
Peter and Mags Desmond
Seán Byrne
Tara Sketchley
Vincent O'Brien
Xander Storey-Cosgrave

We couldn't have done this without your time and kindness. Thank you!

Monstrous
Regiment

🐦 @MonstrousRgmt
📷 @monstrousregiment_
𝘧 facebook.com/MonstrousRgmt/

Monstrous Regiment

Monstrous Regiment Publishing Collective was founded by Lauren and Ellen, two publishing students with a mild antiauthority streak who decided to try to be our own bosses. We're curating the kind of content we want to see in the world: feminist, bold, intersectional, unapologetic and diverse.

The Bible is our inaugural project. Next, we will be launching a quarterly feminist literary magazine in 2018. An official submissions call will be released online, but in the meantime, contact us with pitches at editor@monstrous-regiment.com if you would like to have your writing considered.